THE COLLEGE STUDENT'S HANDBOOK

Abraham H. Lass

AND

Eugene S. Wilson

DAVID WHITE COMPANY

New York

EDUCATIONAL DISTRIBUTOR:
GUIDANCE ASSOCIATES
Pleasantville, New York 10570

Grateful acknowledgment is made to Pocket Books, Inc., for permission to reprint material from *How to Prepare for College* by Abraham H. Lass (New York: Pocket Books, Inc., 1964, copyright © 1964 by Abraham H. Lass), which appears on pages 64-70 and 89-105 of this book.

The College Student's Handbook is available in both a clothbound Library Edition and a paperback Student's Edition. Please write the publisher for further information.

A sound film strip entitled *I Wish I'd Known That Before I Went to College,* based on *The College Student's Handbook,* is available from Guidance Associates, Box 5, Pleasantville, New York.

LIBRARY OF CONGRESS CATALOG CARD NUMBER: 65–17021

DAVID WHITE COMPANY
60 EAST 55TH STREET
NEW YORK, N.Y. 10022

PRINTED IN THE UNITED STATES OF AMERICA

THE COLLEGE
STUDENT'S HANDBOOK

About the authors

ABRAHAM H. LASS is the Principal of Abraham Lincoln High School in Brooklyn, New York and an Education Columnist for the New York *Herald Tribune*. In his many years as an educator he has effectively guided the counselling of thousands of students through the intricate processes of preparing for and gaining admission to college. He is the author of the widely-acclaimed guidance book, *How to Prepare for College.**

EUGENE S. WILSON has been the Dean of Admission of Amherst College in Amherst, Massachusetts since 1945, prior to which for twelve years he was the Dean of Freshmen. He has been a trustee of the College Entrance Examination Board, and a trustee and president of the Association of College Admission Counselors. He is the author of many articles and co-author of the book, *College Ahead! ***

* Published by David White Company, 60 E. 55th Street, New York, New York 10022.
** Published by Harcourt, Brace & World, Inc., 757 Third Avenue, New York, New York 10017.

TO
Betty and Janet
AND
Louise

CONTENTS

INTRODUCTION

EVERY September more than a million students enter America's colleges as freshmen. You will soon be one of them. You have graduated from high school, taken part in community and extracurricular activities, won the approval of your teachers and counselors, survived your college entrance tests and admissions interviews. You're coming to college filled with hope, excitement, and anticipation. You are lucky.

How many of the million or so students who start with you will get what they came to college for—a college degree and, more important, a meaningful education that will prepare them to understand themselves and their times, to find a satisfying career, and to contribute something of value to their fellowmen?

All?

90 per cent?

70 per cent?

60 per cent?

50 per cent?

40 per cent?

Only about 50 per cent of your classmates will graduate on time. About half a million won't. Some will have trouble almost as soon as they get into college. Others will bog down in difficulties by the end of freshman or sophomore year. A smaller number will hang on doggedly only to let go in junior or senior year.

Why? Why? Why? We don't know all the answers. But we

do know some of the most important ones. Not all of them, of course, apply to every one of the 500,000 college drop-outs. But, taken together, they explain why so many able and promising students don't succeed in college:

▶ They aren't trained to work on their own, to set their own goals, to plan and manage their lives.

▶ They can't read fast enough or well enough to handle the college's demanding reading program.

▶ They don't know how to study, how to take notes, how to use the library.

▶ They don't know what to do with their new freedom. They think that freedom means having nothing to do and all the time in the world to do it.

▶ They don't know what they came to college for. They don't see where their studies are leading them.

▶ They are in the wrong college. They chose it without seeing it or knowing what it was like. For them it is too hard, or too easy, too far from home, too confining, too strange, too uninteresting, too lacking in cultural experiences and activities.

▶ They came to college for the wrong reasons: family pressure, friends going, the prestige of the college, low tuition, closeness to home, desire to meet boys or girls, or "nice people," "the right people," etc.

Many drop-outs will return to college, complete their courses, get their degrees, and pursue useful, productive careers. Some, on the other hand, will find that college isn't really for them after all. They will reshape the pattern of their lives and go on to work that is better suited to their special needs and abilities.

We are convinced that most drop-outs need never have dropped out at all. They could have found success and satisfaction in college if they had been adequately prepared for college, if they had only known what college would really be like, what it would demand of them, what problems they would encounter, and how they could solve them.

This is why we wrote this book—to give you a clear, easy-to-understand notion of:

What will happen to you in college from the day you enter until you graduate
What it takes to succeed in college
How to handle your personal, social, financial, and scholastic problems
How to avoid the difficulties that many college students run into.

We have put into this book everything we have learned in a lifetime of teaching, counseling, living with, talking with, and listening to students. All the advice and suggestions gathered here have stood the test of time and experience. Over the years they have worked for thousands of successful college students. They can work for you, too.

The problems that you will meet in college are old problems. They have been around for a long, long time. When you meet them for the first time, they will, of course, seem fresh, new, challenging, and sometimes disturbing. Most of the answers that we have tried to supply are old, too. We hope that you won't shy away from them simply because they are old. You won't find the answers to all your problems in this book—or anywhere else. For some problems there are no ready-made answers. You must find out for yourself which answer is best for you.

The college years, we all want to believe, should be filled with a special kind of happiness and fulfillment. But it's not likely to turn out this way—and you wouldn't really want it to. For problems and challenges that you can meet and solve are the yeast and spice of life. College can guarantee you only an opportunity to grow, to learn, to discover.

You will get out of college what you are capable of getting. We hope that this book will show you how to make the most of your abilities. We hope, too, that it will make you want to know more about more and more, and that with all your knowledge and understanding you will get a bit of that precious stuff called wisdom.

A. H. L.
E. S. W.

THE COLLEGE
STUDENT'S HANDBOOK

CHAPTER 1

YOU'RE IN!

Y ES, *you are in!*
You know this for you have already received that long-awaited letter of acceptance from the Committee on Admissions. Your family and friends have showered you with congratulations and admiration. The labors of the past four years have paid off and you are pleased, mighty pleased, that you are now guaranteed an opportunity to get a college education.

But wait a minute. You are not really in yet. Read that letter of acceptance again. Take a careful look now at a sentence you hardly noticed the first time you read the letter. It goes something like this: Your acceptance is contingent upon three things: (1) your continuing your good academic work; (2) your graduating with your class; and (3) your continuing to merit all the nice things that your principal, counselors, and teachers have said about you.

Each year in June colleges do reject students they have tentatively accepted earlier in the year. Colleges take this action for two reasons: either a student's final-semester marks fall considerably below his record for the previous three and one-half years; or misbehavior in class, at a senior class dance, picnic, or at some other school event calls forth the official disapproval of the school authorities. Colleges are slow to gamble on students whose behavior in high school suggests that they aren't ready to handle successfully the much greater freedom of college life.

1

They have enough difficulty with students with good behavior records.

YOUR COLLEGE

Now high school graduation has come and gone. Your character and marks have not slipped. Your diploma is in hand and you are ready to think seriously about approaching this great adventure called college.

Which college accepted you? Was it your first choice, your second, or your third? Or were you accepted through one of the clearing centers, such as the College Admission Center in Evanston, Illinois? In that case you may be headed for a college you know little or nothing about. We hope you won't waste time trying to rate the college you are entering or contrasting its prestige or influence with other colleges. It matters less than you think which college you are going to, for no college has yet discovered a foolproof method for turning adolescents into mature, thoughtful, responsible adults. You can't name a college or university that has not produced unusually successful men and women and a sizable number of failures, too. Colleges don't really "give" you an education. All they give you is an opportunity to exercise and develop your particular talents and powers, a chance to grow in awareness of yourself and the world around you.

So go to the college which has accepted you, confident that you will find there the teachers, the books, the equipment, and the experiences that will open new vistas of knowledge and understanding to you. Remember, no college can confer fame or fortune on its graduates. No college can guarantee greatness to its students. Prestige has never yet been transferred automatically from a college to a student. A graduate, however, can bring prestige and distinction to any college.

Wherever you go, you will become what you are capable of

becoming. *The only limits placed on your accomplishments will be set by your own interests, aptitudes, resolution, and dedication—not by the college you attend.* Learning is an act of discovery and discovery comes only to the curious, to the questing.

YOUR COLLEGE SPEAKS

Some time in May or June, your college will begin to communicate with you in an attempt to facilitate your transition from school to college. Read these communications carefully and respond promptly and thoroughly to all directions. You are now laying the foundation for the kind of comments and recommendations your college will some day present on your behalf to an employer, to a graduate school, or to the Armed Forces. Each year high school seniors handicap themselves by misplacing letters of instructions from colleges, by a careless disregard of deadlines for replying to questionnaires, or by sloppy and incomplete replies.

Colleges vary greatly in the amount and kind of communications they send. You may receive an elaborate certificate of admission signed by the president. This may be just a custom of the college or a sincere indication of its real interest in you. You won't know which until you have lived on the campus for a while.

If you are an athlete, you will probably hear from a coach. If you have musical talent, don't be surprised to receive a letter from the director of the band, choir, or orchestra. You may even get a letter from the head of the mathematics department or some other academic department, telling you about the great opportunities in that area of study—especially if you have already indicated where you are thinking of majoring. Once again, you will have to wait until you have spent some time on campus before you can tell whether the professor who wrote the letter is desperately trying to revive a faltering department or is speaking for a lively, imaginative group of teachers who are proud of their offerings.

We suggest you keep all correspondence in a file and take this file to college with you. You may want to call on the writer of some letter for further information. He will naturally be pleased if you begin the conversation with a reference to his interesting letter. This simple thoughtfulness will certainly not handicap you at the start of your college career.

Much of your correspondence will come from the Dean of Freshmen. He is the specialist in freshman affairs. He knows the kind of problems freshmen encounter and he knows who can be of most help to you. He knows the teachers who instruct freshmen, their abilities, their interests, and their attitude toward freshmen. He wants to help you have a successful first year. Take your problems to him without fear or shame. If he is a good dean, he won't solve them for you, but he will help you help yourself.

Many institutions have a "Big Brother" or "Big Sister" program in which an upperclassman who has been assigned to help you in your first year begins by writing you a personal letter during the summer before you go to college. The kind of letter you get will tell you much about your older guide. This "pen-pal" relationship sometimes initiates a lasting and rewarding friendship, but don't count on it too much. Acknowledge the letter and ask any questions that you'd like to have answered. When you meet Big Brother or Big Sister you will learn whether you can expect anything worthwhile to develop from this association in the years ahead.

We heard of one subfreshman who had three Big Sisters, but we still don't know whether some mechanical sorting machine just stuttered a bit or whether every freshman in that college had three Big Sisters.

In some colleges, fraternities conduct serious summer recruiting or scouting programs. You may be subjected to inspection by these fraternity advance scouts who want to see where you live, what you look like, how you speak, etc. Your attitude toward secret societies will determine to some extent how cordially you receive these scouts.

If you don't pass this first inspection by fraternity or sorority scouts, don't be too distressed. You will have another chance when you get on campus. Remember, too, that these organizations often judge you chiefly on such qualities as social poise, appearance, background. Secret societies are not for everybody. On most campuses today they do not exercise the power and influence they once did. In any event, you, like many before you, can survive and get a fine education without joining a fraternity or sorority.

You may also get letters from merchants in the college town, who want to "help" you get off to a proper start. Don't rush to make any early purchases by mail. Wait until September when you can buy what you really need and see what you are buying.

Some of the letters you receive from your college may raise questions. Don't hesitate to write and ask for the answers. Remember that your intelligence is often measured by the questions you ask.

CHOOSING A ROOMMATE

One of the early queries from your college will deal with the question of roommates. Do you want a single, double, triple, or quadruple rooming arrangement? List in order of preference but be prepared to get your last choice. Colleges want to give you what you want, but, alas, they have to fit your class into existing dormitory arrangements. If there is a shortage of dormitories, you may have to find, with some help from the college, a room in the neighborhood. We warn you that any similarity between the room pictured in the beautiful illustrated booklet sent to applicants and the room you get is likely to be accidental. Some dormitories are old and some new. The freshmen are usually put into the older buildings. Cheer up. The roof will keep you dry and you won't have to haul your own water and firewood, as students once did.

One of your first college tests, and one for which you will get no recorded mark, will be of your ability to live with a group of your fellow students in close quarters under continuously noisy conditions. If a friend who is cooperative, understanding, and unselfish is also going to your college, try to sign him up quickly and then notify the college that you have a roommate. If you have no such friend, the college will assign your roommate or roommates. Since you are going to live with someone you don't know, you may as well get all the benefit possible from this experience, so ask for a roommate whose race, nationality, or religion differ from yours. If you are an athlete, ask for a would-be poet, and vice versa. One of the major purposes of a college education, hopefully, is to challenge your inherited and acquired beliefs and prejudices. You can put yours to the test by exposing yourself to human beings with different interests and backgrounds.

Most colleges do not have many single rooms, but if some are available, you can request one. Some students shy away from single rooms for fear that they may become lonely in them. But this is hardly likely, for dormitory living is, by and large, a goldfish-bowl existence. Generally speaking, however, we think you'll be better off with a roommate.

CHOICE OF COURSES

One of the precollege tasks you may be assigned is that of selecting the subjects you will take in freshman year, and especially in the first semester. Your selections will not be irrevocable, for you will have an opportunity in the early weeks of college to make necessary changes in your program.

Before you whip out paper, pencil, and catalog and proceed to list the subjects you want, take time to review your reasons for going to college. The answer to the question "Which courses?" lies more within you than in the catalog. What you give in interest and industry to any course is often more important than which course you take or why you are taking it. If your primary purpose in attending college is to develop your personality (become better rounded), or to find a mate, it probably matters very little which courses you take, since most of the important things that will be happening to you will be outside the classroom. If you want a broad liberal education or a general education, then sample generously the major fields of learning before you settle upon one in which you will concentrate the major portion of your time and energy. Unless you are taking a vocational course, ignore those prophets who urge you to embark on courses that "will do you some good after college." No one knows what will do you good later on. We know a law-school student who claimed that an undergraduate physics course was of greatest value to him in law school, and a medical student who said that his freshman required composition course had helped him most in medical school. You never know.

All good courses require you to do three things—collect, cogitate, communicate:

Collect information and knowledge through the eye by reading, the ear by listening, and the hands by working in the laboratory.

Cogitate to assess and sort the information you have collected so you can give order, unity, and meaning to your newly acquired knowledge.

Communicate your knowledge and thoughts in discussions

with your professors and fellow students, and through papers, tests, etc.

Upperclassmen often choose teachers rather than courses, but freshmen are seldom in a position to do this. If, however, the catalog lists the names and addresses of upperclassmen, you will find it helpful to visit those who live near you, to get a view of the freshman academic program as well as other aspects of college life.

At almost all colleges you will be required to fulfill certain course distribution requirements—for example, one course in mathematics or the natural sciences, one in the social sciences, one in language, literature, or the arts, etc. But colleges differ in their placement of courses in divisions of the curriculum. At one college, psychology may come under the heading of science, and at another, of social studies. With one eye on distribution requirements and the other on occupational requirements, choose your program for your first two years. These selections are only tentative; you may change them during orientation or at the end of each semester.

In the preceding paragraph we suggested that you keep one eye on your occupational requirements. And we mean *one* eye—not both. Certain occupations require a heavy program of sequential courses: among these are agriculture, accounting, business administration, art, music, and engineering. But for others you can prepare with a variety of educational programs. Medical schools require only about one fourth of your courses. Admissions committees at the most popular graduate schools of law and business usually do not care whether you majored in the sciences, social sciences, language, or humanities. They are much more interested in what you have done in your major field and what kind of person you are. (See Chapter 14, After College, What?)

We are convinced that all too often students are urged to

make a choice of vocation before they have had an opportunity to discover their own interests and aptitudes and to explore the many jobs and careers they might be fitted for. At a well-known liberal arts college, as many as 20 per cent of students shift from mathematics and science to humanities. Between 5 and 10 per cent of the language and English majors change to mathematics and science. So don't make the mistake of deciding too early and too hastily what you will be happy doing for the rest of your life.

A liberal or a general education does not usually prepare you for a special occupation, but leaves you ready to be trained for many. It also enables you to change jobs or fields of work if you discover you don't like what you are doing. Most people change jobs at least two or three times in a lifetime. Sometimes students who concentrate too early in one vocational field discover when they begin to work that the field is overcrowded, or the job they prepared for no longer exists, or they are getting no satisfaction out of what they are doing. So they seek employment in another area. A general education makes this shift possible.

Curriculum planning begins with you, your interests, your aptitudes, your personality, your expectations. Since your knowledge of occupations and curriculums is limited, you should check your thinking and planning at each point with an experienced college counselor. For all students, whatever their vocational goals may be, we recommend as broad and general an academic course as possible. Whatever you do in the future, this kind of program will keep doors open for you. It will not handicap you.

PRECOLLEGE READING ASSIGNMENTS

More and more colleges are asking or requiring their freshmen to read one or several books during the summer before they come to college. Then, during orientation period or the early part of the first semester, discussions of this material are led by faculty or upperclassmen. This assignment is an opportunity for you to show what you can do on your own. We suggest you read the assignments twice, once when you get them and again the week before you leave for college, and that you make some notes during your readings. If you live near some members of your new class, you might find it interesting to meet once or twice to discuss the reading and its significance.

WHAT TO TAKE WITH YOU

Less than you think, and if you are a girl, still less. We have little hope that anything we say on this subject will influence your decision to any noticeable degree. We have packed sons and daughters off to college and we know, particularly with our daughters, how fruitless were all appeals to common sense, reason, or even emotions—the emotions of the parents.

You know that in rural colleges dress for boys and girls is not only often very informal but at times downright sloppy. Urban institutions usually demand more formal attire. At coeducational institutions dress is more formal than in institutions for males only or females only.

So take the clothing you think will fit the customs of your new community. Count on the mails to take care of the returns and of the forwarding of the things you forgot or overlooked.

For room furnishings, study the catalog carefully to see what the college provides. Some institutions give you only four bare walls, though this practice is disappearing. Second-hand stores usually flourish near any campus, but there are never bargains at these stores during check-in week in the fall.

Since the names of your roommates are usually sent to you in advance, you should check with them to decide who will supply such standard items as bookcase, easy chair (if there is room for one), floor lamps, curtains, rugs, etc., as well as who will provide a radio, record player, or television set.

Many colleges have arrangements with a commercial supplier to pick up soiled sheets, pillowcases, towels, etc., once a week, and deposit clean ones at the same time. Washing machines and dryers also are frequently available in dormitory basements. If you don't mind unironed sheets, pillowcases, and towels, you can save money by using this equipment.

Rules on electrical apparatus in dormitories are sometimes very strict; so investigate these before you bring grills, refrigerators, hair dryers, etc.

However carefully you prepare your list, you will certainly forget something. You will also take many things you will never wear, need, or use. Again, the mails will save you.

Books, especially science books, are expensive; so ask for the list of books required for the courses you plan to take the first semester. If you live in or near a large city, you may save money by purchasing these at a second-hand bookstore, provided you can obtain the latest edition of the required books. Inquire about the availability of second-hand books on the campus. If you patronize the college second-hand bookstore, buy early, for there are never enough second-hand books for all. Don't plan to save money by sharing books with roommates. Though it may net you some small initial savings, this is not usually a satisfactory arrangement. Own your own books.

YOUR FIRST WORRIES

As the weeks of summer pass and the day for departure draws nearer, most freshmen find themselves somewhat apprehensive about college. Can I pass that required math course? Will I fail history (I never could retain all those facts and dates)? How will I ever cope with beginning French?

Then there are other worries about "making good," "being

liked," "getting homesick," etc. Why shouldn't you have such worries? They are perfectly natural and understandable. College is a big step into the unknown. For centuries freshmen have worried when they were about to take this giant step. But don't worry about being worried. The right kind of worry is normal and healthy. It makes you act when you should act; it makes you think hard about what you are doing and should be doing. Remember, too, that many of the things you worry about will never happen. Your college is confident that you can handle its academic challenges and adjust to all other demands, too. Trust your college's judgment and the ability of its staff to help you meet the challenges of college life.

CHAPTER 2

ORIENTATION

ALMOST all colleges set aside a few days or a week before classes begin for what is known as "orientation." Though your entire precollege life has been, in a very real sense, orientation and preparation for college, each college wants to try in its own way to ease its students' transition from school to college.

OBJECTIVES OF THE ORIENTATION PERIOD

Colleges differ greatly in the length, intensity, and variety of their orientation programs, but running through all these programs are these common objectives:

To make you feel welcome
To acquaint you with the physical characteristics of the college
To introduce you to individuals who can help you
To check the appropriateness of your academic program
To obtain through special tests (yes, more tests!) information about you which will be used in counseling you and placing you in proper courses.

Here are some ways in which colleges and universities accomplish these objectives.

13

MAKING YOU FEEL WELCOME

Whether you come to the campus by car with your family or alone by train, plane, bus, or subway, you will probably find that the Registration Office, the dormitories, even the transportation centers are swarming with Big Brothers, Big Sisters, or others, marked by name tags and identified often by colored armbands, who are ready to lead you to your proper destination. These friendly, attractive-looking, hand-picked people welcome you and your parents and, with little difficulty, erase any doubts you may have had about the wisdom of your college choice.

At the registration desk or in your room you will usually find a packet of material which will include your orientation program, a map of the campus, tentative course schedules, your name tag, etc.

Before you put on your name tag, consider this the proper moment to record your favorite nickname and to bury forever any unattractive nicknames you may have acquired in high school or earlier. This is the time for "Sneaky Davis" to become "Bull Davis" or "Butch," and "Fatso Rogers" can now change to "Buck." If some ancestral handle like "Hepzibah" has clung to you for eighteen years and you think it limits in some mysterious way the development of your personality, scratch "Hepzibah" and replace it with "Hep" or something more remote like "Ginger." Remember, the nickname you launch now will probably be yours not only for four years, but for the rest of your life. So choose with an eye to the future.

Impressed as you may be by all the attention of upperclass students, don't let their friendly welcome turn your head. Next week, when classes start, you will be on your own again. That nice, warm, friendly junior who was so good to you and your parents will probably pass you on the campus without a hint of recognition. And why not? She greeted fifty-five newcomers in those first two days. And that pleasant faculty member or adviser who called you by your first name when he checked your course schedule will probably give you a vacant stare when you meet in the snack bar. Again, why not? He has twenty-five other freshmen to counsel, six hundred and fifty students in three courses, and fourteen graduate students to guide. His failure to call you by name does not indicate a lack of interest in you, but more probably a deep absorption in the many problems which arise at the start of a new year. Or he may just be nearsighted!

Short-lived as the interest of the student greeters may be, you do know you were expected, and you do know a few upperclassmen by name, upperclassmen on whom you may call for help if and when you need it. Though these upperclassmen may not call you by name on campus, their interest was not entirely artificial. When you stop them and remind them of the help they gave you on that first day, they will be ready to help again. Go to them if you need them.

Sometime during that first day on campus you will receive an official call from your resident dormitory adviser or proctor, who may be an upperclassman or a faculty member. He will inform you of the location of his quarters, give you a printed list of rules for dormitory living, and urge you to call on him for any help you may need. More about him later.

Welcoming greetings will be extended by upperclassmen if you are in a college that mixes in each dormitory first-year students and upperclassmen. If your college houses freshmen in separate dormitories, you will feel welcomed by the sheer excitement of all the surrounding freshmen as they mill from room to room, exchanging names, home towns, whom-do-you-know's, and other vital statistics.

Included in your registration envelope is a map of the campus. Tuck this into your pocket and keep it handy, for you will use it daily for the first few days—or weeks—depending on the size of the campus and your ability to memorize the location of key spots.

Campus tours will probably be organized by some upperclass honor society, often with special stops at the library, art museum, theater, laboratories, and gymnasium. Take advantage of these tours, for they give you an introduction not only to the geography of the campus and the equipment in special buildings but often to key faculty personnel.

Some colleges organize special tours for students with special interests, i.e., a visit to the astronomy building for potential astronomers or astrophysics majors, a visit to the music center for students with vocal and instrumental aspirations, or a call at the theater for budding actors and actresses and the technical experts who back them up. These special tours are a "must" for all students with burgeoning or developed special interests and talents.

Your college may not provide separate tours for students with special interests and talents. If this is so, round up a few classmates with interests similar to yours and make a call on the department, where you will surely find a professor, a graduate student, or even an upperclassman who will be delighted to know of your interest in his special field and who will give you and your friends not only a guided tour of the department but a lecture on the importance of this area of study in "these crucial days of the world's history." Should there be no freshmen near you who share your special interests, try putting a notice on the dormitory bulletin board, giving objective, time, date, and place for the start of such a tour. A phone call to the department requesting permission for your invasion (giving date and time of arrival) should be made to insure a proper reception for your own organized tour.

In managing your own tour you risk being kidded by your classmates for being the managerial or executive type. Don't let this upset you. All too often students sit around and wait for someone to do something for or to them. Your initiative may inspire other students to do some research and investigation on their own.

This new college you are in is now your college. Take time out during orientation period to explore and investigate. Discover as much as you can about the opportunities which surround you. Don't wake up in senior year, as many students do, and then ask, "Why didn't someone tell me in freshman year that *that* was here?" or "that *he* was teaching English?"

INTRODUCING YOU TO INDIVIDUALS WHO CAN HELP YOU

By the end of the first day you will have met two of the key helpers in your academic life, your Big Brother or Big Sister and your dormitory adviser or proctor.

These are key individuals, not so much because they themselves have the knowledge and experience to handle all your problems as because they know where you can go to get the special help you may need. Do not hesitate to seek information and, at times, advice from them.

You and your classmates will be introduced during one of the class meetings to the chief college officials: the president, deans, chaplains, etc. For all freshmen three administrators are particularly important: the Dean of Freshmen, the college physician, the chaplain of their faith. The chaplain will help you with problems associated with your religion; the college physician will treat your physical ailments—and sometimes your emotional problems, though usually students with emotional problems will be referred to a clinical psychologist or a psychiatrist. The Freshman Dean will discuss your academic problems with you, though he may also refer you to any one of your teachers. Some teachers are skilled counselors.

During orientation period you may or may not meet the financial aid officer. Most colleges have a specialist in this area who can help you solve your financial worries, whether they be about jobs, loans, how to manage a budget, how to handle a checking account, etc. If you don't have unlimited resources, make a special note of the financial aid officer and the location of his office. Don't be afraid to discuss your problems with him. He is paid to listen to your tales of financial need and to work out a program through which you can help yourself.

You will meet students who say they can *help* you, and at times they will. But most of them swarm around you to assist you in exchanging some of your good hard cash for objects you supposedly need. These upperclass salesmen often try to sell freshmen everything but the clapper in the chapel bell and, history tells us, even this item has at times been sold to gullible freshmen. With the famous Latin phrase *caveat emptor* (let the buyer beware) indelibly imprinted in the back of your mind, welcome each salesman warmly and with interest, for some of them do have bargains for freshmen. After hearing what they want to sell, ask yourself: Do I need it? Can I afford it? If the answer to both of these questions is yes, then ask one more question—why at this time?

The following items are most often offered to freshmen by upperclassmen:

Second-hand books. Before you jump at what may look like a great bargain, check the prices with the regular second-hand bookstore and make certain the professor who used this book last year is again requiring it. Many freshmen learn too late that the book they have just bought has been replaced by a more timely revised edition or a different book.

Second-hand furniture. The first week of college finds all second-hand furniture, whether offered by upperclassmen or local merchants, at top prices. Wait if you can, and do with what you have. Prices fall steadily throughout the year and usually take an abrupt drop a week after college has begun.

Second-hand electrical equipment. Radios, shavers, clocks, irons, etc., may be offered in abundance by students trying to pay off some summer debt or to unload worn-out pieces. You can get bargains in electrical goods if you know the equipment, the seller, and the real reason for selling. If you do buy from students, get a written one-month guarantee of satisfactory operation.

Clothing, old and new. On second-hand clothing, you probably run little risk of entrapment. On new clothing, ask the upperclass salesman whether he sells with the college's approval or without. Most colleges try to keep clothing salesmen out of the dormitories because they undercut the local merchants whose taxes help support the college. Most colleges require students with commercial affiliations to register with a college official. If the student has official approval, you are then free to weigh the merits of his product.

Miscellaneous items. Included here are such diverse articles as desk blotters and blotter holders, beer mugs with the college seal or name, college pennants and stickers, alarm clocks, and books of coupons good at local stores. Again, let your needs and your finances control your desires. You don't have to buy on the first day. If you like an article but don't want to purchase it at once, take the name and college address of your friendly salesman and tell him you will get in touch with him later. He will probably mutter something about his short supply or about higher prices later on, which may or may not be true. You are on your own now. Remember, there are very few items which can't be purchased later at the same price or even at a lower price, once the college year has begun. Sometimes if the friendly salesman discovers that he is stuck with an extra supply of beer mugs or school calendars you can help him unload later on in the fall at your own price!

CHECKING THE APPROPRIATENESS OF YOUR ACADEMIC PROGRAM

Most colleges require you to present your academic schedule or program to a dean or faculty adviser for final approval. Your faculty adviser will have reviewed your secondary school transcript and your test scores to make sure that you are taking courses you can handle. He will inquire about your educational goals and he will check to see that your program will lead you to these goals. He will also want to make certain that the courses you have selected are open to freshmen, that they meet the distribution requirements set down by the college, that they give you the proper credits for the first semester, and that no two courses meet on the same day at the same hour.

If you have good reasons for taking a special program that does not conform to the published requirements for freshmen, ask your adviser if you can postpone until sophomore or junior year a requirement that is blocking your choice. Most institutions do have some flexibility and do make exceptions to stated requirements, provided, always, that the reason for the exception is sound.

You will have one more opportunity to make changes in your program (see "Courses," in Chapter 3, Freshman Year).

Once your academic program is approved, get a course schedule card from your adviser or the Registrar. These cards show which hours and days of the week the various courses meet. On this card you can write in each hourly space the name or the number of each course, where it meets, and the name of the teacher.

As soon as possible, get your campus map and find the rooms and buildings where your classes will be held. Time the distance between the buildings so that you will know whether to walk, trot, or run to classes in the first week.

OBTAINING INFORMATION ABOUT YOU

Sometime during orientation period your college may set aside time for tests: aptitude, interest, achievement, personality, etc. You can relax as you take these tests! Your future is not at stake. The results of these tests will: (1) help your counselors place you in the correct academic sections, especially in English, mathematics, and languages; (2) give important information about you to educational and vocational counselors.

SOCIAL EVENTS

Scattered through most orientation programs are certain special social events such as receptions, teas, student "mixers," etc.

FACULTY RECEPTION

Many small colleges have a special get-acquainted reception for faculty and freshmen. These affairs can be stiff and boring, especially for freshmen nervous about approaching professors who sometimes gather in groups exchanging greetings with their colleagues and gossiping about life since last June. This is a time to summon up your courage and address a strange professor with "Excuse me, I'm a freshman. My name is John Jones. What do you teach?"

From this gambit you will probably get the name of the teacher and he will probably play the where-are-you-from, whom-do-you-know game. Your follow-up questions may lead to a lively chat with an interesting teacher.

The important point is that you should take the initiative. Some teachers are hesitant about introducing themselves to freshmen and will welcome your overtures.

FACULTY ADVISER'S TEA

Many colleges assign freshmen to individual faculty members, six, twelve, or twenty students to a teacher. The latter often invites his advisees to his home for a get-acquainted tea. Whether these affairs are fun and entertaining or deadly dull depends on the professor and on your attitude and actions. Be sure to take a few questions with you. They will start the conversation. Arrive on time and have no hesitation about departing when your instinct tells you it's time to go. This is your move, not the host's.

A thank-you note to your host and hostess after the tea is proper.

STUDENT "MIXERS"

These evening affairs are not confined to co-educational colleges, for men's and women's colleges, too, make a great effort to have their boys or girls meet some "nice boys and girls" from institutions nearby (up to 100 miles).

These affairs are wonderful or awful, depending on what happens to you. They are wonderful if you dance with more than one partner, if you can exchange words with several members of the opposite sex, and if you manage to make a follow-up date with a congenial person. But they are awful if you get stuck with the wrong partner, find yourself tongue-tied when you do meet someone attractive, or remain a "wallflower" most of the evening.

One hint to the male reader. Be bold and adventuresome. The cute-looking girls will all get a big, steady rush. If you cut in, you won't have enough time to mutter your full name before someone else cuts in. So try gambling a little bit. Go to the sidelines and ask some "plain Jane" to risk a dance with you. If no lights flash, say a nice "thank you" when the music stops and try another gamble. On one of these you may discover a lively mind and personality and, when you do, you have a head start on the pack who won't know what you know until far into the semester.

The sparkling, pretty girls have their own special problems and sometimes are not worth the fight you will have to get some of their time. Similarly, girls, beware of the handsome "All-American" boys. They can be very unreliable, and, if you are going to get them, the chances are that a "no" will keep their interest much longer than a "yes" will.

For most students the college-sponsored mixers of early freshman year are a disappointment. Students who have been going steady in high school find they can't talk to strangers of the opposite sex as easily and naturally as they had hoped, and either become awkwardly wordless in their distress or begin babbling on in a loud, affected way. Students who have not been going steady in high school too often hope the mixer parties will immediately produce a steady. In this hope, honest, natural young people sometimes assume a pose which may get a steady, but one who won't be steady long.

Students who are still going steady with someone back home when they come to college should consider returning all symbols of love undying, such as class rings, gold footballs, pins, etc. Freshman year in college is not, in our experience, the best time to go steady. It is a time for exploration, for meeting many different types of the opposite sex, for testing, if you will, the depth of the foundation of your previous love. If your high school love is the real thing, it can probably stand exposure to a variety of dates. If it can't stand this test, you had better discover this at eighteen instead of at thirty-eight.

FRATERNITY AND SORORITY RUSHING

Although the present trend is toward deferred rushing, many institutions permit fraternities and sororities to pledge freshmen during the orientation period. Where this custom prevails, an additional strain is placed on many members of the freshman class.

We know of no way to make you happy about not being pledged if you think membership really important. We could, however, tell you about men and women who were not "good enough" to be chosen for social groups in freshman year and who, by senior year, had become class officers and leaders. We could recount true stories about very successful college graduates who, as undergraduates, were not "good enough" to make a fraternity. We could remind you, too, that your teachers and the books you read won't know or care whether you join a fraternity or not.

If you are disappointed by rejection, we suggest that you refrain from displays of bitterness or aggressive attempts to please rushing chairmen, and that you continue to be yourself. Throw yourself into your studies, find an activity, confident that your worth as a person will be made manifest in time.

Our years of observation of students accepted and rejected often give us more concern for the accepted (especially the most sought after), because they sometimes believe they are really better human beings than those not chosen. This sense of superiority, this ego inflation, can retard the growth, development, and education of a student.

To many students, the orientation period often seems too long and too dull. If the period seems dull to you, you had better re-examine yourself carefully. There is so much to investigate on any college or university campus, so many new people to meet, things to do, that the student who finds himself bored during orientation period will probably be bored not only throughout college but all through life.

CHAPTER 3

FRESHMAN YEAR

TOMORROW classes start!

You are in your dormitory room seated at your desk. Before you on the desk are a map of the campus and your course schedule for the week. You know you can make each class on time because you have located each building and checked the walking time from classroom to classroom. On the right-hand side of your desk is an awesome pile of books which are required for the first semester. You won't have to carry all of them to class as you did in high school. You smile as you recollect the way some of your classmates looked as they struggled down the high school corridors, bent into crescent shapes by their load of books.

Your first class is at 8 A.M. So you set your alarm clock for 6:30, allowing ample time for dressing and breakfast.

You now turn out your lights and go to bed. Sleep comes slowly as you try to fight off the doubts about your ability to survive successfully in this new world. Those books on the corner of your desk, dimly lit by the campus light, look big and ominous. Your classmates look much brighter than you expected them to. The upperclass men and women you have met seem so poised and confident. You can't help wondering.

Relax. Remember that after studying your four-year record, your intellectual and vocational aspirations, your test scores and your references, the Admissions Committee was convinced that you could be successful if you worked.

Like all your classmates, you will have many new problems, in the classroom, in the dormitory, and around the campus. Many of these problems you will be able to solve alone or with aid from your classmates. Others may require more experienced heads. No student is ever fully prepared for all eventualities.

This chapter will touch upon the major problems that all students in all types of colleges encounter in their first year in college. We can't solve all your problems for you. But we hope that we can give you an understanding of the nature of what lies ahead of you and prepare you to face and handle your problems effectively.

INSTRUCTORS

As former instructors and as administrators in educational institutions where we have many friends who are instructors, we naturally think of instructors as patient, industrious, dedicated men and women. We know that students often think of instructors in these terms, too. But we also know that there are times when, for a student, an instructor can be a problem. When we talk of instructors as problems we are not placing them in any special position, for, in the same sense, parents are problems, bosses are problems, top sergeants are problems.

Instructors are people. They come in all sizes and shapes of body, mind, spirit, and ability. You will generally not be able to choose your instructors. You will have to work with those assigned to you. And make no mistake about this: it is your job to get along with the instructor, just as it is a private's job to get along with his superior officers and an employee's to get along with his boss. You don't have to like your instructor but you do have to work for and with him.

Your instructor doesn't have to like you and he does not

have to get along with you. His job is to teach you—to introduce you to the pleasures and rewards of learning.

Learn the names of your instructors. Many instructors write their names on the blackboard at the first class meeting, but many do not. Some give their names orally to the class, clearly and distinctly, spelling the name if it is an unusual one; others mumble their names. Get the name, the full name, from the instructor or the catalog and write it in your course notebook. Under his name write his office address and campus phone number. You can also list his home address and phone number, but forget these except in dire emergency. Instructors do not as a rule remember kindly those students who invade the privacy of their homes without invitation.

Call your instructor by his name rather than "sir," and use "professor" rather than "mister." He may not be a professor in rank but you can call him professor without offending him.

Before the first week is out we suggest you find out all you can about your instructors, their methods, attitudes, and idiosyncrasies.

Attendance. Find out early how your instructor feels about your attendance. Instructors differ greatly in these matters. Some don't care whether or not students attend classes while others take an absence as a personal insult.

Most colleges have adopted an institutional policy on class absences or cuts, which is usually stated in the catalog. But not all instructors like or agree with institutional policy. We know students who have had difficulty when they tried to live by an institutional policy which did not require class attendance when the individual instructor wanted his students to attend all his classes. As one such instructor said, "I work hard to prepare for my classes and I don't expect to lecture to an empty classroom."

If your instructor resents absences, don't cut. If he doesn't care whether or not you come, do what you think best.

Tests. Here again instructors hold a variety of views. An instructor should announce at the start of a course the kind of tests he will give and when they will be given. Students should know whether they will be asked to take objective tests or essay tests. Some instructors use unannounced or "police" tests to encourage attendance, especially in institutions where there is no requirement for attendance. Others use this type of test to encourage students to complete the weekly reading assignments.

We like to think that all students work for the joy of discovery, the excitement of learning. But we know from long experience that the number and type of tests a professor gives do influence the kind of emphasis a student will place on his study and review. Some instructors stress the memorization of many minute facts and isolated data. Others are more concerned with your understanding and interpretation of major trends, events, ideas, facts, etc.

We recently talked to an honor graduate who had received her only C in four years of college in a second-year language course in the field in which she was doing her honors work. In answer to our inquiry about the reason for this one low grade, she said, "Well, I met an instructor whose main interest was in grammar. Since I was more interested in the ideas in the materials we were reading, the instructor and I did not exactly mesh on results."

If you can't or don't know how to discover your instructor's attitude toward tests, ask some sophomores who have taken the course.

Marks. Teachers also differ in their attitude toward marks and in their marking practices. Some instructors mark a student each time he participates in a classroom discussion. Others encourage participation but make no attempt to assess performance. Some instructors place great weight on the results of surprise quizzes, while others don't even record these marks. The marks for papers assigned during the term may count anywhere from one-third to one-half of the total term's mark. Unless there is a school-wide policy, instructors weight final examinations differently, too.

Unfair as it may seem, some teachers distribute their marks on a strict curve (from A to F) regardless of the ability of the students. Other instructors give each student what he deserves even if this means giving all A's and B's. Some instructors don't believe in failing students, and others seem to believe that their professional integrity demands failing from 10 to 30 per cent in each term.

We know that you have your own views about marks. And they may be very valid views. But your teachers are not obligated to agree with them or accept them. So find out what marking standards your instructors are following and guide yourself accordingly. (See page 37 for more on marks.)

Students. To some few instructors students are a nuisance. They are interested primarily in writing and research. To most teachers, however, students are partners, junior partners to be sure, in the exciting enterprise of learning.

We urge you to make no snap judgments about your instructors' attitude toward students, for so varied are teaching methods and philosophies that you can easily be wrong. It takes time and thought to judge a man fairly. Some instructors seem unnecessarily cruel, harsh, sarcastic, and punitive in their words and actions, but this is often done on purpose, to jar you into thought and action. Measure your teacher's attitude toward you, not by what he says or does, but by what kind of thought and action he produces in you and your classmates.

Your instructor's greatest challenge is to increase your desire to learn. An experienced instructor knows that some students can be inspired by a pat on the back, some by kindly, encouraging words, others by sarcasm, ridicule, or even harsh criticism.

In speaking as we have been about instructors' attitudes we don't mean to imply that learning is a kind of game in which the student tries to "con" or outsmart his instructors. Most instructors are aware of the artful practices of student entrepreneurs and know exactly how to deal with gamesmanship. They know as well as anyone the variety of interests, techniques, and objectives that exist in any group of teachers. They respect students who accept these differences.

If you use your knowledge of your instructors' personalities, techniques, and expectations properly, you will get real pleasure (and better marks) in your courses. But don't permit this special knowledge to lead you into short-cuts in your preparation or into artificial attempts to please your instructor.

There are no short-cuts to learning, no easy paths to intellectual discoveries. Learning is hard work—work you must do on your own.

COURSES

Your first introduction to the problems of course selection probably came during the summer when you received from your college a list of course offerings and requirements for freshmen. At that time you made tentative selections which you reviewed with an adviser during orientation week.

Now you are in the first few weeks of college and you know from experience what your instructors and courses are like and what demands will be placed on you during the first term. You may discover that there is little similarity between a course as it is and as it was described in the catalog. You may find, especially in mathematics and foreign languages, that you are placed in a section that is either too advanced or too elementary for your ability and experience.

If the pace and demands of a course are beyond your capacities, hustle over to your faculty adviser or your Freshman Dean and state your case. If you are not really overplaced, your adviser may be able to help you understand why you are in that course or what you can do to meet the demands of the course. If he agrees that you are overplaced, he will help you select a course you can handle. If you are in a course you can't cope with, the sooner you discover it the better. Consult your adviser at once.

In most colleges, courses may be changed by a student any time during the first two to six weeks, though there is sometimes a fine for these late changes. Your catalog will probably give details about course changes or you may find the answer in your freshman handbook. After six weeks, many colleges will not permit you to drop or change a course without penalty. In some colleges, however, you can drop a course any time up until the final term examination, but you will find your transcript marked "wp" (withdrew passing) or "wf" (withdrew failing). In other colleges you will be given a failing grade (40, for instance) if you drop a course after four or six weeks.

Your courses will be handled in a variety of ways. You may, for example, have an all-lecture course, a part-lecture, part-discussion course, an all-discussion course, some of which may also have laboratory or seminar sessions.

In your all-lecture courses, be prepared for different approaches. One instructor will carefully outline his lecture either on a blackboard or in mimeographed notes, while another will give neither outline nor notes. One instructor will have his material well organized and another will have little apparent organization. One instructor may talk clearly and rapidly and another may mumble and talk very slowly. One course will stress coverage of a vast amount of material and another will call for an understanding of the basic concepts and principles of a small amount of material.

Since most high school courses are not lecture courses, many college freshmen have difficulty in adjusting to this kind of teaching. They find the problem of note-taking especially troublesome. (See Chapter 9, How to Take Notes.)

In some large colleges and occasionally in small colleges, too, enterprising students reproduce for sale the notes of popular lecture courses. Resist the temptation to purchase such notes. Learning to take your own notes, to separate the important from the unimportant, is an essential part of your education. Bear in mind, too, that most good lecturers change their lectures from year to year, adding new and fresh material, dropping dated, inaccurate material. The lazy student who is using last year's notes may well be missing something important.

BOOKS

In the chapter on Orientation we mentioned the importance of owning your own books, if there are required textbooks, and the dangers in buying old, used, or second-hand books. You may find yourself in courses which do not use a textbook but which require outside reading from books in the college library. In such courses, reading assignments, which usually supplement the material presented in lectures, generally cover a two- to four-week period. During this time the library copies of the books are placed on a special shelf of the library and reserved for students in the course.

A problem arises here because there are never enough books for all students to read at the same time. Ordinarily, these reserved books must be read in the library reading rooms, though some colleges permit students to take the books out on what is called "overnight loan." They must be returned by 8 or 9 o'clock the next morning.

Don't postpone your required reading until the last day or two. If you do you may not be able to get a book when you want it. This can be disastrous if the required reading precedes a test. We know of no instructor who has ever been moved to clemency by the wail, "I couldn't get a book; they were all in use."

We suggest a careful reading of required work the first day or two after you are given the assignment. Take careful notes. Then review your notes the day before the examination. Such a schedule will guarantee you easy access to the books you will be required to read or consult.

STUDY

In talks with hundreds of failing students, we have been surprised to discover how often the roots of their failures lay in poor study habits and skills; their ignorance of how to read a book, what to read, how to take notes, how to use the library, how to prepare and write a long or short paper, how to review for an examination. Apparently it is possible for high school students to graduate with good marks and not really know how to study properly. We have devoted special chapters to these problems (Chapters 5-11).

ROOMMATES

Problems involving roommates usually fall into one of two categories, solvable or unsolvable.

Here are some typically unsolvable roommate problems:

▶ One likes four hours of sleep and the other eight.
▶ One likes to sleep with the windows wide open in winter and the other wants the windows closed tightly.

▶ One loves the music of Bach and the other wants only jazz.
▶ One thinks the room is for entertainment for students; the other thinks the room is a study center.

If you and your roommate have many such differences, we suggest you try to find more congenial roommates right away. Problems like these cannot be compromised easily.

Here are some solvable roommate problems:

▶ One is neat, the other messy.
▶ One likes to study with the radio on, the other wants silence.
▶ One smokes, the other doesn't.

Roommates with problems of this nature have found it helpful to hold a weekly or monthly gripe session to air and discuss their annoyances and differences. Nothing is worse than for one roommate to suffer in silence some idiosyncrasy of the other. It is far better to get grievances out into the open. If you and your roommate can't reach an agreeable settlement, take your problem to the dormitory adviser or the Dean of Freshmen. If the differences between you and your roommate cannot possibly be adjusted, then both of you should ask the Dean for a shift.

One word more about roommates. Don't make a hasty judgment of your roommate if he is someone you have never met before. Some personalities reveal their real worth slowly. By sharing common problems and adversities you can begin to know the person you live with.

We remember an incident at an old New England men's college. On the afternoon of registration, a father, a successful businessman from the Far West, called on the Freshman Dean and demanded that his son be given another roommate. When the Dean asked, "Why?" the father said, "I won't have my son rooming with a New York Jew."

The Dean asked the father to describe a New York Jew. The

father said, "I know your tricks and I am not going to discuss this further. Change my son or I'll take him to another college." As the father stalked out of the office, the Dean said, "Leave this matter to your son and I'll discuss it with him."

The next day the Dean invited the son to his office. When he told the boy that his father had called the previous afternoon, the boy, without hearing more, said, "I know, but don't worry about him."

At the end of the first semester, the Dean asked the freshman if he wanted to change his roommate for the second semester. The freshman said that not only did he want to keep his original roommate, but that they were planning to room together the next year. The Dean never heard from the father again.

The greater the differences between roommates the greater the opportunity to discover the fact that all men and women have fundamentally the same fears, hopes, needs, and aspirations. Harmonious coexistence with another personality of the same sex requires (and this also applies to married couples) an ability and desire on the part of both individuals to change the changeable and to endure the unchangeable with patience and good humor.

SPORTS AND ACTIVITIES

One of the great myths that persist in high schools is that all students who want to impress admissions committees must present a long list of achievements in sports or other extracurricular activies. Only these students, it is thought, will seem well-rounded enough to win admission.

The myth hangs on in colleges, too, and moves students to undertake sports they dislike, activities that bore them, all to convince parents, peers, and potential employers that they are not "grinds," but well-rounded men and women of the world.

Just when the colloquial appellation "grind" was born we do not know. We suspect it was an antonym for the type of student who got a "gentleman's C" from his instructors. Today the public acclaim given top students by awards of state and national scholarships has almost rendered the word "grind" obsolete and made the top scholars the golden students of this age.

We don't mean to imply that sports and extracurricular activities are a waste of time or that they have no educational value. For most students they are important for several reasons:

► They provide an outlet for talents that are not used in scholarly pursuits.

► They require teamwork and cooperation and act as an antidote to the self-centeredness of learning. College years are the years when young men and women are freest to forget everyone's needs but their own, the years when they are rarely required to make a significant personal sacrifice.

► They afford students a change of pace from the daily tasks of learning. Few indeed are the students who can find pleasure and excitement only in constant intellectual endeavor.

The freshmen are most likely to be trapped into excessive involvement in activities because they often volunteer for an activity without investigating the time demands it will make and before they know how much time and effort their studies will require. A good rule for most freshmen is to try out for only one activity or sport and then only after carefully exploring how much time and energy they will have to give to it. The activity should be one for which the freshman is qualified and which he will enter for the simple joy of doing and not to gain popularity or recognition or to please parents or fraternity brothers. In your first year be sure you have enough time if you plan to engage in any of these activities: dramatics, singing groups, radio stations, campus publications, and free-lance dance-band combinations. Student leaders of these activities may try to sweep you into the group by promises that you will have to play only a minor role that will demand little of your time. But our experience has been that, once you join, an "emergency" is quite likely to arise which will call for your maximum assistance. Now you are trapped. Your sense of loyalty to your organization, which your "friends" will not hesitate to emphasize, will persuade you that you can let your studies slide for a while. So move slowly when the time comes to consider athletics or extracurricular activities.

MARKS

With one exception, marks are a problem to instructors and students alike. The apparent exception is of course the student who gets only high marks, but, ironically, marks are often a problem to the straight-A student too. More about him later on.

Instructors are concerned about marks because they realize how subjectively they judge their students and how slight is the evidence on which a mark is based. Students worry about marks because they feel, and often with some justification, that these marks are not fairly arrived at and do not really reflect what they know and what they have achieved. How often have you heard students comment about marks: "This isn't fair"; "He asked the wrong questions"; "I studied the wrong things"; "This proves he doesn't like me"; etc.

Instructors' marks are at best inaccurate measures of scholastic achievement because there is no national standard of achievement. Marking habits of individual instructors within a college or university differ greatly, and marking habits of faculties in different institutions also vary widely. We know students who have failed at one college and then transferred to another at which they became members of Phi Beta Kappa. We also know a student with an A record who transferred to a college with stiff marking standards and flunked out.

If marks have no universal meaning and if no one likes them, why do instructors continue to use them? Well, marks are old tribal customs and no one has found a satisfactory substitute for them, though many groups and individuals have tried.

Marks may indicate that you have acquired some knowledge, but they do not necessarily indicate that you are any wiser. Marks do not measure your total worth as an individual, nor do they measure your all-around powers and capabilities. Furthermore, they do not, at times, even record accurately your ability as a student.

But if you think that marks are not important, try failing a course or two and see what happens. Marks may not always measure ability and achievement accurately. They may be overstressed, and in terms of a total life they may not be at all significant. While you are in college, however, marks are the coin of the realm and with this coin you acquire honors and recognition. Marks control who gets prizes, who drops out and who graduates, and often who gets into what graduate school. Marks are probably the most important factor in your college career. You ignore this truth at your peril.

Your first college marks, which will probably cover work on short quizzes or papers, will enable you to check your first efforts and also give you some notion of what your instructors want from their students. For example, we remember a freshman who got a zero on his first humanities paper because he twice misspelled "Odyssey," the name of the book his class was reading. He was particularly annoyed because his roommate, in another section of the humanities course, misspelled "Odyssey" three times and still got 92 with red-penciled "sp's" after the misspellings. In this instance, one student learned that his instructor was a stickler for correct spelling. The other student learned that ideas were more important to his instructor than technical accuracy in grammar and spelling.

The first marks in freshman year usually come at the end of four, six, or eight weeks, depending on the practice of the college. Even if these are based on no more than a one-hour test, seminar discussions, or a few short papers, they will give you some notion of your progress, some idea of your weaknesses.

If at this first marking period you are failing a course, try to understand why. Is the course too difficult? Do you lack adequate preparation? Have you studied properly and sufficiently? Can you overcome your problem in this course by your own efforts or do you need some tutoring?

If you can't discover why you are failing, then, as soon as possible, visit your dormitory adviser or proctor, your instructor, or the Freshman Dean. It is essential that you find out immediately how to improve your performance in the course in which you are weakest. All too often freshmen muddle along, hoping that something magical will occur to make things better. There is no magic in learning. Don't expect any.

Some colleges send marks to parents and some do not. Some send midterm marks to parents, while other colleges send only final term marks home. Find out the policy of your college so your letters home can help your parents understand your achievements or lack of them.

Each year in all colleges many freshmen face a downward readjustment of their estimates of their own intellectual ability as measured by marks. High school honor students, and the A student in particular, are usually hit hardest of all. The reasons are many, but the following are dominant:

▶ Most high school classes have students ranging in ability from the lowest to the highest. Only able students are admitted to college. Therefore, whether you were an A, B, or C student in high school, in college you will find many more students whose intellectual ability matches or surpasses your own. The competition is naturally keener.

► In high school, assignments tend to cover short periods of time, i.e., day to day. But in college, assignments may extend over a week or several weeks. This requires an adjustment in planning and thinking that not all students are able to make easily and quickly.

► In many high schools any student with a good memory can get an A. Many colleges, however, are more concerned with the student's understanding and use of knowledge. Hence they reward the ability to think and reason more highly than mere memory. Though memory has a firm place in all learning, some students find themselves slow to adjust to this shift in emphasis.

► There is always a bottom half to every class. Students who attend highly competitive colleges have greater adjustments to make to marks. If there were a college which accepted only A students, probably no more than 5 to 25 per cent of its students would have a college average of 90 or A. It isn't easy or pleasant for students to accept lower marks than they have been accustomed to getting. But fortunately most do come to terms with the college marking standards and see themselves more realistically in relation to their fellow students.

► A students often have a tendency to let their academic success inflate their egos to the point where they think they are not only brighter than other students but better people. Greater knowledge should promote greater understanding and bring men and women closer together. But sometimes learning serves to separate the scholar from his fellow men and makes him an intellectual snob—perhaps the worst kind of all, for he should know better.

► Faculty marking standards vary greatly from college to college. In one college, for instance, 25 per cent of the marks will be A's; in another, 10 per cent. But the admissions committees of graduate schools recognize these differences when judging undergraduates and, therefore, will accept from one college only students in the top 10 per cent of the class, while accepting students in the bottom half from another.

Marks are only symbols of learning, not learning itself. Marks are by-products of learning, not its goal. Concentrate your thoughts and energies exclusively on learning and on the excitement of new discoveries. Even though you must work for marks, remember that ten or twenty years after college your marks will be hidden away in your scrapbook, but your learning will contribute constantly to the richness and meaning of your daily life.

FREEDOM

Ask any college-bound student to tell you where he will have his greatest difficulty in college and nine times out of ten he will mention some academic subject—math, social studies, foreign languages, etc. Rarely will he mention *freedom*. Yet for many students the greatest test is how to use the new kind of freedom they have when they get to college.

The intelligent use of freedom is man's perennial problem and challenge. The problem is magnified for the college student, however, because as a rule he has not had much practice in the use of freedom during his first eighteen years, either at home or in school. Colleges intentionally grant students a generous degree of freedom in the belief that only in freedom can the lessons of freedom be learned. Colleges do have some protective rules for students (more for freshmen than for upperclassmen) but, in the main, there are fewer restrictions in the college years than in the years that follow.

Freedom in college is a test not only because students are inexperienced in living with it but also because the college years present many students with their first big temptations.

In spite of the paternalistic surveillance of the college authorities, students often encounter, for the first time or at least in greater abundance, the traditional destroyers of personalities: wine, women, song, and gambling. For co-eds the dangers are most often wine and men. Paradoxically, the more sheltered and protected the student has been for eighteen years, the greater the stress and strain of the college years.

But the traditional temptations will not be your greatest test. For you it will be the daily choices you must make about using your time wisely. Can you stay in your room to write that important paper when two doors down there is a bull session in full swing on some "hot" topic? When a group of friends stops at your door and says, "Come on to the movies," can you reply, "Sorry. I have some reading to do at the library"? Decisions like these separate the men from the boys, the women from the girls. The ability to say "no" at the right time for the right reasons is the first sign of maturity. It rests on the realization that the mastery of freedom requires tremendous self-discipline. (See Chapter 8, How to Study, for some suggestions on managing your studying and leisure time sensibly and effectively.)

DEPRESSION PERIODS

In all boarding colleges and sometimes in commuting colleges, many freshmen suddenly find themselves engulfed by discouragement, a lack of confidence in their ability to survive, a lack of purpose, and a deep desire to go home or almost anywhere else. There are two traditional periods of depression for freshmen. One comes anywhere from seven to fourteen days after the start of classes and the other one or two weeks after Christmas vacation.

The first depression often has homesickness as its taproot and hits hardest those who are away from home for the first time. Since most students think there is something weak and unmanly about being homesick, the subject is not mentioned in student conversations. This gives a homesick student the impression that he or she is the only one in the class who is suffering from this malady. The truth is that most students who have a real home feel some pangs of homesickness during the first few weeks of college, though they would rather flunk a course than admit it.

Homesickness is usually not a long-lasting or contagious ailment. It never kills anyone nor does it disable anyone for long. Time is the finest remedy.

Homesickness may not be the heaviest contributor to the first depression. The main problem may center in a feeling of personal inadequacy brought on in part by the confident appearance of other classmates, all of whom look much brighter and more competent than you expected them to. Again, the confidence of your classmates is often just a pose. Few freshmen are ready to admit that they are frightened by the academic load or by their strange new surroundings and challenges. Their ego requires a bold display of confidence and assurance.

Other factors contributing to this first depression are: the rapidity with which the lecturers talk, the length of the reading assignments, the difficulty of separating the important from the unimportant in the mass of material presented in reading and lectures, and the varied adjustments that each individual must make in a totally new environment.

We remember an incident that took place in late September on the campus of a women's college in Pennsylvania where a group of counselors from high schools and colleges was meeting. We were talking with a high school counselor when two girls from the counselor's school came up to greet him. To the counselor's question, "How are things going?" both girls replied at once, "Oh, fine." Then both burst into tears and wailed, "We want to go home. We can't possibly do the work they expect us to do."

We tried to help them understand that they were suffering from early "depressionitis" and that this affliction was present in campuses all over the nation. The counselor, because he knew the girls' backgrounds, could reassure them about their ability to keep up with the academic pace at their college.

We made a note of the names of these two girls, and in a follow-up made at year's end found both doing well scholastically and both very happy. They said they were ready to help next year's freshmen overcome "depressionitis."

Pills won't cure your first case of depressionitis. As a rule parents cannot help much either, though parental attitudes and actions may shorten the duration of the affliction. Intense involvement in some academic subject or activity may bring some relief. If the suffering is sharp and prolonged, a frank talk with the Freshman Dean or student counselor may help. If the freshman can't find relief, then he, like a ship at sea, must ride out the storm, firm in the faith that no storm lasts forever and that calm seas and blue skies always follow the winds and rain.

The second depression follows Christmas vacation and hits hardest in those colleges which have midyear examinations at the end of January. This depression comes from academic worry centered on the impending term-end exams, from feelings of guilt about work planned but uncompleted during Christmas vacation, and from the weather, especially in northern states where the first January thaw makes everything messy.

For boarding students the depression is heightened by the great contrast between life at home during vacation and life back at college. At home the family was so glad to see you that you were probably treated like a king. Your father gave you unlimited use of the family car, your mother cooked all your favorite dishes, and those professional tormentors, your little brothers and sisters, treated you with awe and respect. Then, too, your old high school steady was waiting with open arms for you and she looked lovelier and more mature than ever. College was never like this!

When you return to college you can't help feeling slightly depressed, for you are once again carless, your admiring family has been replaced by some critical, grumbling classmates, and, to top it all, on the fourth day back you receive a letter from your girl telling you that she does not love you as much as she seemed to during vacation and that there is now someone else. It seems she was using the Christmas vacation to test her emotional attachment to you, an attachment that had not been tested since last September! "Dear John" letters almost always come as a shock and surprise and they start many a post-vacation depression.

We have no magic medicine to lessen the pain of this second depression. Like the first one, this, too, will pass. A serious methodical preparation for the approaching midyear examinations is an excellent antidote. (See Chapter 11, How to Take a Test.)

If you sail through freshman year with no depressions (there are students who do), be mindful of the needs of your fellow students. Your words and deeds can increase or lighten the problems they face. You, more than anyone else, can help them to overcome their periods of doubt and melancholy.

TRANSFERITIS

A concomitant malady to freshman depression is "transferitis," an itch that infects many students at some point in their freshman and occasionally their sophomore years. This itch is sometimes brought on by glowing letters from friends at other colleges, friends who, paradoxically, may be suffering the same trials and doubts you are suffering. The itch is also aggravated by the age-old human belief that the other field is greener and happier.

We don't mean to suggest that freshmen should not contemplate transfer to another college. There are legitimate reasons for transfer, but these reasons should usually be tested by a full year's work at your first college.

Three good reasons for transfer are:

► You are not being fully challenged academically.
► You are really in a program that is beyond your reach.
► Your college does not offer sufficient opportunities for study and research in the area of your major interests.

If you find you are not fully challenged by your present courses, discuss this fact with your faculty adviser or your Freshman Dean. You may be able to take an extra course in the second semester. If this is impossible, select the course which interests you most and see your instructor in this course about the possibility of doing extra work. You may be able to arrange for additional time in the laboratory, extra reading, or special papers on some topics allied to the course. If your class assignments do not fill your time, challenge yourself with additional work.

If you think the work in your present courses is beyond your capacity, again call on your faculty adviser or dean. He will check your school preparation, your study habits, your test results, and will suggest remedies. You may be allowed to drop a course or to change your program at the start of the second semester. Don't become too discouraged too soon. We have seen many freshmen raise their scholastic average a full ten points between the first semester of freshman year and the end of sophomore year.

The suggestion that you give your present college a full year's test does not apply to those students who clearly lack the ability or the incentive to complete the first semester satisfactorily. Such students after consultation with the proper authorities should drop out or transfer as soon as possible to a college where they will be able to function better. Many students, however, give up too soon. Don't fall into this error. Don't abandon your college plans until you have discussed them with your instructors, advisers, and dean, and until all indicators clearly point to the *out* sign.

Our talks with hundreds of transfer applicants reveal the interesting fact that most of these students make similar complaints: the instructors are dull and incompetent; the attitude of other students is nonintellectual; there is no quiet place to study; the work is not challenging. Since these applicants came from many different colleges and universities we assume that there are some common student complaints about all colleges and that changing colleges will not necessarily eliminate the complaint. What we often suspect, however, is that the applicant is telling us more about himself than about the college he attends. The interested, industrious student will find a quiet place to study, fellow students who are stimulating and intellectual, work that is challenging, and teachers who are not boring.

If you believe you have a legitimate reason for transfer, we suggest you try to spend at least one day on the campus of your "new" college and that during this day you live the life of a local student, attending classes, eating in the dining room, and talking to students. Such an investigation has cleared up more than one case of transferitis and has allowed a restless student to see that the rich green-looking field over there is really only a hayfield.

If it is not possible for you to visit the campus of the college you wish to transfer to, then, at vacation time, call on the undergraduates who live near you. You can get their names from a catalog or from the registrar or public relations office of the college you are considering. Try to find out all you can about the college: the kinds of students it accepts, the standards it sets for them, the number and quality of courses, the teachers, the facilities, living and study conditions, etc.

The transfer itch is most prevalent between Christmas and spring vacation. Again it has been our experience with students from many colleges that this malady is short-lived and clears itself up between spring vacation and the year's end. There is something healing in soft spring breezes, the full moon of May, and the beginning of some real friendships. Our counsel, except for students clearly overplaced or underplaced, is to stay where you are unless come May you still itch all over.

There are other legitimate reasons for transfer. A change in your family situation (health or finances) may demand that you return home and attend a nearby college. Your college may be too religiously or too secularly centered to suit your needs or point of view. No matter why you want to transfer, test your thinking with your parents, friends, teachers, and counselors. Allow a little time to pass before taking the final steps.

The problems we have discussed in this chapter are the major ones that freshmen usually meet. Whatever problems you face, if you can't solve them by yourself, seek the aid of those around you—other students, dorm proctors, instructors, faculty adviser, Freshman Dean, counselors, and the medical department. For many reasons most students would rather suffer with their problems than discuss them with anyone else. This is not intelligent. On your campus are men and women who have had experience with all kinds of student problems and want to share this experience with you. When your heart is heavy with worry, seek help. This is not the time to be proud or stubbornly independent.

CHAPTER 4

MEETING YOUR
FINANCIAL PROBLEMS

WE DID not include the problem of finances in Chapter 3 because it is not exclusively a freshman problem. When you came to college, you had a plan for paying for your college education. You and your family had budgeted your income and expenses for each month of college. In spite of such planning, there are few students who don't at some time find themselves hard-pressed to meet some financial need which arises out of faulty financial calculations, sudden changes in family financial conditions, or unexpected college expenses. Whatever the source of the problem, the need for money exists and you have to take some steps to meet it.

WHO CAN HELP YOU?

There are various individuals who can help you when you face a major or minor financial crisis. We suggest you approach them in the following order.

You. The first question to ask yourself is what you personally can do about your financial problem. Have you been managing your money wisely? Have you been extravagant? Begin by reviewing your financial planning and your budget. What steps can you take now and in the months ahead to cut down on

49

expenses and make up the deficit which faces you? Is the need which brought on the financial crisis a real need or an imaginary one? For instance, are fraternity or sorority dues your problem? If so, can you postpone membership for a year?

If you can't solve your financial problems alone, then you must turn to others.

Family or relatives. Your parents may be able to help. If they can't, they may know of some relative who has always been interested in you and would like to help you through this emergency. It isn't often, however, that relatives can save you. In preparing to send you to college, your father and mother probably canvassed the assets in the coffers of relatives. Since most families have to budget very closely to put any one child through college, it is probably unlikely that you can get additional help from home.

Financial aid adviser. If neither you nor your parents can find the money you need, see your college financial aid adviser. He is an expert who knows all of the varieties of student aid available in and outside the college community. Take your problem to him and place all the facts before him. He will explore with you the possibilities of scholarships or financial aid awards, short-term loans, jobs around the college or in the community, and various money prizes awarded annually to outstanding students.

While you are with the financial aid adviser, ask about loans or scholarships from all the organizations with which you or your family have been associated: civic, social, religious, and fraternal organizations, and such groups as the 4-H Club, Boy Scouts or Girl Scouts, and labor unions. Many of these organizations maintain scholarships, grants, and loan funds for members or for sons and daughters of members. You may be eligible for aid from one or more of these sources.

Teachers and coaches. Your financial aid officer may be able to tell you which of your teachers or coaches can help you.

Sometimes they know about special funds. For instance, if you are a Latin scholar, your Latin teacher may have access to funds available to students whose work in Latin is outstanding. If you're in the band, the band director may know of alumni or organizations who are particularly interested in helping key members of a band. If you have a strong record in sports, your coach may know of some legitimate way to obtain alumni support, or he may be able to tap some special fund for your needs. Naturally you will approach only those of your teachers or coaches with whom you have a close personal relationship and for whom you are doing outstanding work. More than once a teacher or a coach has been able to help a student when everyone else has failed.

You again. You have tried everyone and everything and you have not been able to get the aid you need. What now? You are alone with your problem as you were in the beginning. Don't give up. There are still other avenues to explore. Your financial aid adviser had no jobs to offer you, but in your college community, whether it is a small country town or a big city, there are people who need help and who are willing to pay for this help. You will have to use your own methods to locate them.

If you can type, you will probably be able to find an administrative officer, teacher, or local businessman who needs extra help. Then there are always classmates who can't type and who will pay you to type themes and term papers.

Babysitters are always in demand in every community. Talk to your teachers, to the minister of the church you attend, to the students who run the babysitting program. Put an ad in the college paper and local newspapers.

In a large city restaurants, hotels, and department stores often need extra help Saturdays and Sundays. Read the Help Wanted ads and register with local state and federal employment agencies.

We know of one student who got a nightwatchman's job from 11:00 P.M. to 6:00 A.M.—a job which required him to sit at a desk and be prepared to answer a phone for forty-five minutes of each hour. The other fifteen minutes were set aside for punching clocks around the warehouse. Since the warehouse was filled with a heavenly quiet all night, the student was able to do his studying while on the watchman's job. He slept in the afternoons. The job paid his expenses.

Another student got a job when no job seemed to be available by sending a double postcard to the full professors and associate professors on the faculty of his college, which was in a small country town. He offered to rake lawns, wash windows, clean attics, and do miscellaneous household chores, at $1.25 an hour. The response from his mailing was so great that he hired two other students at $1 an hour and pocketed a quarter for each hour that his assistants worked. At the end of three weeks he had worked himself out of his financial jam.

There are jobs around. You can find them by using some initiative and imagination.

WHEN YOU CAN'T GET HELP

You've tried every source mentioned here, and you have talked to every expert available. You can't get a job and you can't get further loans to meet your financial needs. What can you do now? What many college students in a spot just like yours have done—drop out of college for a semester or a year. Get a job. Work to pay off your financial obligations and put aside some money to take care of your expenses when you return to college. You are coming back. That's why you're leaving now—so that you can come back with enough money to see you through.

Before you leave, talk to the Freshman Dean about your present situation and your future plans. If you are doing good work in college there is always a slight chance that he may find some way for you to continue through the second semester. If not, you can arrange with him for the proper temporary termination of your academic work and the resumption of your schedule when you return.

Don't go away from college feeling sorry for yourself. Many students have been forced to take this drastic step in order to get the education they want. From a job you will learn many things which will give added meaning to your studies when you return. You won't be wasting your time.

Whatever you do during your leave of absence, on your return college will seem more precious than ever before.

CHAPTER 5

HOW TO USE
THE LIBRARY

THE college library is one of the first places you should visit and get to know. Here over the next few years you are going to do some of your most important work. If you don't use (or aren't required to use) the library regularly and intensively, you will be missing something vital in your college education.

We remember so well the remarks made by a student who was dropped in freshman year for poor work. He took a turn in the Armed Forces and was readmitted. At the end of the first semester after his return, his average was 85. So marked was the difference between his academic record before expulsion and after return that we called him in to ask what had happened. His answer was: "The library is the difference. When I came here the library was an assignment. Now it is an opportunity."

You can't possibly own or buy all the books, magazines, and reference materials that you will have to read or consult. If you aren't looking beyond your textbook, if you aren't searching the records of the past and the present for information, insight, and understanding, you are not being fully educated. We are not suggesting that you spend *all* your days and nights in the library. You would certainly emerge fantastically knowledgeable if you did. But you'd have too much of a good thing too soon. We do, however, feel very strongly that if you are to get all that college has to offer you, you must:

Acquire the library habit. If you aren't already a thoroughly confirmed library-goer and library-user, start becoming one now.

Get to know the library's basic facilities and personnel—the kinds of books the library stocks, where they are, special departments and services, library hours, library procedures, whom you can call upon to assist you with your problems, etc.

Many libraries issue special student library guides which tell you all you need to know about the library and its program, how it operates, what it is prepared to do for you, and how you can most profitably make use of the resources.

A word about librarians and the library atmosphere. Librarians know and like books. They like reading them and handling them. They like students, too. They like serving them and helping them. Don't hesitate to approach them with your problems. You will find a warm, helpful welcome. The well-run library is quiet. That's the way it should be—a place to read, to study, to do research, to be alone with your thoughts in the specially hospitable setting that only the library provides. Cherish and respect those who create and maintain this haven for you.

WHAT YOU WILL FIND IN THE LIBRARY

Everything in the library is carefully, ingeniously arranged and organized so that in a matter of minutes you can get exactly the book, magazine, pamphlet, periodical you want. Though college libraries do not all follow the same classification system, they all contain certain basic devices and materials.

THE CARD CATALOG

Here you will usually find three cards for each book: an author card, a title card, and a subject card. They all contain the same information about the book. The three-card system is intended simply to make it easier for you to find a book when you know:

The title, but not the author
The author, but not the title
The subject, but not the author or the title.

On the catalog card you will find the following information:

Call number.   This tells you where to find the book. If it is in a special collection or not on the open shelves, you will have to fill out a call slip. The call number, which you write on the slip, will enable the librarian to find the book for you.
Name of author—last name first
Date of author's birth (and year of death if he is no longer alive)
Title of book
Publisher
Date of publication
Number of pages in book

INDEXES TO PERIODICALS

For your term papers and other kinds of research, you will frequently need up-to-date information which you can't get from any book. Books, especially those dealing with the current scene, tend to get out of date. Furthermore, what you are looking for may not yet have found its way into a book, because it is either too new or too special and limited in its appeal. You will therefore have to consult files of newspapers and magazines. You will generally be able to find what you are looking for in one of the following indexes.

Reader's Guide to Periodical Literature. This is probably the most widely used index. All its listings are by author and subject. It carries, in addition, a valuable cross-reference index. If your library doesn't have the periodical you need, it may be able to borrow it or a microfilm copy from another library.

International Index to Periodicals. Materials in this reference work are listed by author and subject. It includes many learned, professional, technical, and humanities journals not indexed in the *Reader's Guide.* It lists foreign as well as American periodicals.

The New York Times Index. The materials listed here, by subject, have appeared in *The New York Times* since 1913. *The New York Times* is, by common agreement, one of the world's most comprehensive as well as most objective newspapers.

Special indexes. These are geared to meet the needs of specialists in such fields as art, agriculture, education, engineering, psychology, etc. If your researches take you into any highly specialized or technical area, find out whether your library has a special index that you can consult. Try the departmental library, too. Here you can frequently get the book or periodical you need, or at least a few good leads.

Indexes for abstracts. These contain summaries of books and articles written in special fields. These abstracts serve a most useful purpose. By reading an abstract you can tell at a glance whether there is anything in the book or article that you can use. Among those available are *Biological Abstracts, Chemical Abstracts, Psychological Abstracts,* etc.

GENERAL REFERENCE BOOKS

Most of these should be familiar to you. If you haven't handled them at all thus far, make it a special point to spend some time learning how they are put together, the material they cover, and how to use them most efficiently.

Encyclopedias—general. These range from the one-volume *Columbia Encyclopedia* to the multivolume *Britannica*. They are continually revised. Supplements are issued regularly to all libraries and private subscribers. The most widely used encyclopedias are:

> *Encyclopaedia Britannica,* 24 volumes
> *Encyclopedia Americana,* 30 volumes
> *New International Encyclopedia,* 27 volumes
> *Columbia Encyclopedia,* 1 volume
> *Collier's Encyclopedia,* 20 volumes
> *Catholic Encyclopedia,* 16 volumes
> *Jewish Encyclopedia,* 12 volumes

Special encyclopedias. These include:

> *Encyclopedia of the Social Sciences,* 15 volumes
> *Harper's Encyclopedia of Art,* 2 volumes
> *Encyclopedia of Educational Research* (Walter S. Monroe, editor)
> *Van Nostrand's Scientific Encyclopedia*

Yearbooks. Some of these, like the *Information Please Almanac,* you can purchase quite cheaply. Yearbooks deal (almost exclusively) with current events and personalities, information about trade, governments, etc.

> *American Yearbook*
> *Britannica Book of the Year*
> *Information Please Almanac*

World Almanac and Book of Facts
New International Yearbook
Statistical Abstracts of the U.S.

Dictionaries. If you can afford it and if you have space in
your room, by all means get an unabridged dictionary. It
naturally contains much more than even the best desk dictionary. But most of the time a good desk dictionary will serve
you adequately. When it fails you, use the unabridged dictionary in the library. The following desk dictionaries are the
most frequently recommended:

American College Dictionary
Webster's New Collegiate Dictionary
Thorndike-Barnhardt Comprehensive Desk Dictionary
New College Standard Dictionary

The standard unabridged dictionaries are:

*Webster's New International Dictionary of the English
    Language*
Oxford English Dictionary, 13 volumes
New Standard Dictionary of the English Language
*Webster's New World Dictionary of the American Lan-
    guage,* 2 volumes

Special dictionaries. These are extremely useful source
books. Among the most widely known are:

Bartlett, John. *Familiar Quotations*
Stevenson, Burton E. *Home Book of Quotations*
Fowler, H. W. *A Dictionary of Modern English Usage*
Roget, P. M. *Thesaurus of English Words and Phrases*
Webster's Dictionary of Synonyms and Antonyms
Webster's Biographical Dictionary
Webster's Geographical Dictionary

CHAPTER 6

HOW TO READ

A GREAT many college students don't read well enough to keep up with their assignments. And they don't get all that they should out of the reading they are able to do. How then do they manage in college? Some, by pushing themselves as hard as they can, just about keep their heads above water. Others don't understand everything they read and don't always get through their required reading. So very early in their freshman year they begin falling behind. They will be having trouble all through college. Still others are overwhelmed by the kind and amount of reading they have to do. They quickly flounder and drop out. College is just too much for them.

Of course, many college students stand up pretty well under the challenge of the new reading demands. But, at first, even they have some difficulty handling all their required and supplementary reading.

Very few students go through college without running into some reading trouble. Naturally, the better student will have comparatively few reading problems. The less able student will be plagued by more.

YOU CAN READ BETTER

Is there anything you can do to improve your reading abilities? Without a doubt. The experts say that practically anyone can learn to read better. How much better? That depends very much on what is wrong with his reading, how long he has been having reading difficulties, how hard he is willing to work to improve his reading. Then, too, every reader has his limits. He can't go beyond these limits no matter what he does. But very few of us have reached our limits, are reading as well as we can. So no matter what your reading is like now, you can do something to make it better.

WHAT KIND OF READER ARE YOU?

You have part of the answer. You know whether you are keeping up with your work. You know, too, how much you understand of what you read. The results of formal reading tests will give you additional information about your reading strengths and weaknesses. Your instructors can be very helpful to you here.

The following two checklists should provide you with a fairly accurate picture of your reading assets and liabilities. If, after you have all the information you can get, you're still not clear about what's right and what's wrong with your reading, consult a reading expert or a reading clinic. But be sure that the expert or the clinic is recognized, accredited, and reputable. The shady "expert" or "clinician" will do you more harm than good. Check each individual or agency with your counselor, your adviser, the chairman of the psychology or education department, or the person in charge of reading instruction.

WHAT IS THE GOOD READER LIKE?

► He reads easily and rapidly.
► He understands what he reads—readily and fully.
► He remembers what he reads.
► He reads with a purpose. Before he starts to read, he knows

what he wants to get out of his reading: facts, ideas, answers to questions, pleasure, etc.

► He reads groups of words—"thought units."

► He reads rapidly or slowly, adapting his reading speed to his reading purpose and the kind of material he is reading.

► He has a wide, varied, accurate vocabulary. He keeps adding to his vocabulary.

► He reads critically. He does not accept anything he reads without first questioning its accuracy, validity, motives.

► He reads all kinds of materials in many fields.

► He enjoys reading.

WHAT IS THE POOR READER LIKE?

► He reads slowly and haltingly.

► He does not understand much of what he reads.

► He quickly forgets a great deal of what he reads.

► He seldom knows why he is reading. He has no reading purpose.

► He reads word by word, frequently going back over what he has read.

► He moves his head from side to side while he reads, points at the words with his finger, moves his lips, says each word out loud or to himself.

► He reads easy and difficult materials at the same speed—slowly.

► He has a skimpy, inadequate vocabulary. He rarely looks up words in the dictionary and does not know what to do with the meanings of words he does look up.

► He is a limited reader. He sticks to one or a very few kinds of reading matter.

► He reads comparatively little. He doesn't like reading and for the most part reads only when he has to.

HOW TO IMPROVE YOUR READING

*Set aside a specific time each day (or every other day) to practice your reading skills.** You won't improve much unless you do this job regularly and systematically.

Don't allow other activities to turn you aside from the job you have set yourself. If you can manage to resist the first few distractions and keep to your determined course, you'll find it easier and easier to start and get through with these skill-practice sessions.

Concentrate on the materials especially designed to help you improve the skills you are deficient in—or to develop skills you don't have.

Don't get discouraged. There will be times when you won't seem to be making any progress at all. When this happens, you will probably be on what the psychologists call a "plateau." You may be at this level for some time, but then suddenly

* The following books contain useful, practical practice materials and suggestions:

How to Become a Better Reader by Paul Witty (Chicago: Science Research Associates).

Better Reading in College by Martha Dallman and Alma Sheridan (New York: Ronald Press).

Efficient Reading by James I. Brown (Boston: D. C. Heath and Company).

Better Reading and Study Habits by Victor H. Kelley and Harry H. Greene (New York: Harcourt, Brace and World).

If your college has a reading laboratory or is conducting an active reading program, it will have some or all of these books available for you to consult. You should be able to get copies from a public library or the college library. But if you possibly can, purchase the ones that seem best suited to your needs. These books are meant to be studied and worked with, especially the reading passages and practice exercises. The authors approach students' reading problems thoughtfully, soundly, and reasonably. Simple, intelligible step-by-step analysis of the reading skills you need to succeed in college is followed by carefully selected reading passages, each of which calls upon you to exercise one or more important reading skills. Self-checking tests enable you to discover the progress you are making.

you will again find yourself reading faster and better—but only if you keep working while you are on the "plateau."

Increase your "mental capital." Read widely. Go to movies, plays, lectures, concerts. Listen to what is good and stimulating on radio. Watch TV when it is worth an intelligent person's while to watch.

Keep honing up your reading skills on your regular, required course reading. Try to apply to this important reading what you learn in your practice sessions.

When you are practicing to improve your reading speed, use interesting, not too difficult materials, such as newspaper or magazine articles, "light" novels, essays, or short stories.

Do your reading in a noise-free, distraction-free place. Be sure the lighting is adequate and free of glare (see Chapter 8, How to Study, page 92).

HOW TO BUILD A VOCABULARY

You can read only as much and as intelligently as your vocabulary will let you. Every word you know, recognize, and can use is an idea or series of ideas. The larger your vocabulary, the more ideas you have to think with and about, the more you can understand of what you read. With a limited vocabulary you are a limited reader. With a rich and expanding vocabulary, you can read easily, widely, and deeply. Naturally, you will need more than a good vocabulary to become a good reader. You will have to master certain basic reading skills. (More about these later in this chapter.) But all these skills are built upon your vocabulary.

Here are some practical, workable suggestions for developing your vocabulary. But first a few words of warning about how not to build a vocabulary:

Stay away from books, schools, or individuals who promise

to give you an enormous vocabulary in a matter of days or weeks. In two weeks, you'll get two weeks' worth of vocabulary. That's all—and it's small pickings, indeed.

Stay away from those long lists of words that someone tells you have appeared or are likely to appear on College Board, National Merit, or other kinds of scholarship or entrance examinations. Both claims are likely to be only partially true at very best. Trying to memorize lists of isolated words is probably the least successful approach to vocabulary building. The easiest way to forget a word is to study it the way the list-makers recommend you do. No one is likely to acquire a useful vocabulary this way.

So don't be panicked or fooled into spending your time and money on any kind of get-rich-quick vocabulary schemes that guarantee to make you a word-wizard overnight. None of them work.

Then why do so many people get enticed into these schemes? Partly because they're ignorant and gullible. They just don't know any better. Partly because, being too lazy and maybe a bit foolish, they believe what they want to believe—that they can get something substantial without really having to work for it.

There's only one safe, reliable way to build a large, useful, responsive vocabulary: by working at it all the time, slowly, patiently, and intelligently. It takes a lifetime to grow this kind of vocabulary. But there's no drudgery or dullness involved in building a vocabulary. Every new word adds something to your understanding of yourself, of the people and the things in the world around you. Every new word gives you another avenue of entry into the world of books and ideas. Every new word you master enables you to communicate with others with greater clarity and vividness.

Your vocabulary is a living part of you. You think, act, talk, read, and write with your vocabulary. Like all living things, it must be fed if you expect it to grow and stay sturdy and healthy. Here are a few hints on the care and feeding of your vocabulary.

Read more and better books. (See Chapter 7, What to Read.) Don't waste your time with inferior books. They are written for limited minds—and perhaps by limited minds, too. You'll learn few, if any, new ideas or words (which stand for ideas) from the kind of book properly labeled *trash* or *junk*. The good books and the great books (you are ready for both) are written in rich, stimulating, memorable language by men with something to say about ideas, events, places, and people worth writing about and reading about. The systematic and careful reading of good books is the best single method for developing and enriching your mind—and, automatically, your vocabulary.

But reading alone won't do the trick. You will be meeting new and interesting words in your reading. You will have to do something to get at their meaning and make them your own.

Develop the dictionary habit. Buy yourself a good, reliable desk dictionary. Any of the following will serve your purposes: *Webster's New World Dictionary, Webster's New Collegiate Dictionary, American College Dictionary.*

Look up all words whose meanings you don't know. But don't interrupt your reading to look up unfamiliar words unless, of course, you can't understand what follows. Most of the time, you can come fairly close to getting the meaning of a word from its context—from the sentence in which it appears or from the preceding or following sentences. This kind of guessing is, of course, no substitute for knowing exactly what the word means. So check the word you've guessed at and look it up after you've finished your reading.

When you look up a word, be sure to note:

Its original meaning (generally set down in brackets immediately following the word).

The present meaning or meanings of the words. (Many words have more than one meaning. You don't have to learn them all.)

Which meaning (if there is more than one) of the word applies in the specific sentence where you found the word. For example, "run" has a great many meanings. But only one would apply in this sentence: "Maris hit his fifty-first home *run*." You would have to examine the various meanings of *run* until you came upon the *one* that best fitted this sentence.

Keep a vocabulary notebook. Enter in it all the new words that you come across, the original sentences you found them in, and the dictionary meaning that applies to each. In the beginning, you are likely to find yourself looking up a substantial number of words. This is to be expected. But as your vocabulary grows, you'll naturally have fewer and fewer words to look up.

Learn some common Greek and Latin roots, prefixes, and suffixes. English is a "reservoir of classical languages." About 25 per cent of our words are in one way or another derived from or related to the Greek. Another 50 per cent are of Latin origin. But you don't have to be a Greek or Latin student in order to recognize the Greek and Roman ancestry of the words you use and meet. There are a number of selected lists which you can easily master in a short time. One such list can be found in the *Century Vocabulary Builder.** Knowing something about where words come from increases your interest in and command over them.

Develop an interest in the origins of words. Words are living

* Garland Greever and Easley Jones (New York: Appleton-Century-Crofts, Inc., 1922).

things. They are born, they grow old, some die. And sometimes they are born again. You'll find an interesting and entertaining treatment of the fascinating history of many of our words in *How to Build a Better Vocabulary.**

Maintain a lively interest in the world around you. You'll increase your vocabulary almost automatically. Changes in our ways of living and behaving, scientific discoveries, political and social developments, all bring about five thousand new words a year into our language. Many of these words drop out. But a goodly number become a permanent part of our language. Words like *astronaut, cosmonaut, automation, nuclear energy, jets, countdown* are relatively recent arrivals. But they are already as familiar to us as *TV, radio, supermarket,* which were new words just a few years ago.

Become a word collector. Pick up the unusual, colorful, picturesque, vivid words in your reading and use them. Savor them for their exceptional sound or meaning or appearance. Look into their backgrounds. Find out where they came from and how long ago. Then use them wherever you can in your speech or writing, but always correctly and appropriately.

Here are a few of the words that attracted us when we began collecting words in high school: *dulcet, limpid, brusque, grotesque.* We're not sure what drew us to these words then— possibly the spelling, and certainly, in *dulcet,* the sound. But it really didn't matter. They started us on a lifelong romance with words. We hope it happens to you.

Learn to use a thesaurus (a rather unusual but attractive-looking old Greek word for *storehouse* or *treasury*). When we speak of a thesaurus today, we refer to a unique book of synonyms, antonyms, and related words. The thesaurus is an indispensable tool for anyone who is building a vocabulary. It

* Maxwell Nurnberg and Morris Rosenblum (New York: Popular Library).

is not a dictionary. It doesn't take the place of a dictionary. Nothing can take the place of a dictionary. It is, however, one of the most useful and exciting books you can own if you're interested, as you should be, in enlarging your vocabulary, extending your mastery over words, and expressing yourself with force and precision. The *Thesaurus* comes in many editions. There's a special paperback edition we think is just right for you. It's put together so you can use it easily. We think you'll find it one of the most rewarding investments you have ever made: *Roget's Pocket Thesaurus* (New York: Pocket Books, Inc.)

When you learn the meaning of a new word, learn a few of its synonyms and antonyms. These are usually given at the end of the dictionary entry. The synonym-antonym method is an easy and highly effective way of acquiring whole *families* of words every time you look up *one* word. But handle these words with care. *Synonyms* are very similar to, and *antonyms* are the opposite of, the original word. Both, however, express various *shades of meaning.*

Develop a basic vocabulary list for each of your subjects. Keep adding to it as you learn new facts, concepts, and relationships.

Add a few new words to your vocabulary each day. If you do all the reading you should—good books, good newspapers, good periodicals—you should have no difficulty finding at least five words you don't know. Looking up the meanings of these words should take you about fifteen minutes. Simple arithmetic will tell you that at this easy-to-take rate you can add 1,825 new words (and 1,825 new ideas) every year!

Words belong to those who use them. Your vocabulary won't grow if you just look up unfamiliar words and add them to the growing list in your notebook. That's only the first step in the development of an active vocabulary. Once you've gotten the word down, you can make it really your own by:

Making up sentences with the word.

Using it in your compositions, reports, papers, letters.

Using it in your conversation. Your friends may be a bit startled at first, especially if you've always been talking in colorless monosyllables. You may be in for some short-lived, good-natured kidding. Take it in stride. It's all in a good cause—a richer, fuller, more expressive vocabulary for you. Your friends will get used to your new vocabulary and admire you for it, just as they've gotten used to other changes in you.

HOW FAST SHOULD YOU READ?

Faster than you are now reading. How do we know? Simple. Most people don't read as rapidly as they are really able to read because:

▶ They don't know they can read any faster.

▶ They can't see why they should read faster.

▶ They don't realize that they are getting less reading done because they can't read faster.

▶ They have acquired a set of bad reading habits that keeps them from reading faster.

▶ They have been taught or believe that the slow reader is a better reader, that the fast reader is a careless reader. Wrong, of course. Actually, the fast reader is generally the better reader. Some good readers are slow readers; most are not.

WHY READ RAPIDLY?

Your required and supplementary college reading schedule is a heavy one, probably two to three times as heavy as your high school schedule. You don't have twice or three times as much time to do this reading. But your instructors will nevertheless expect you to get it done on time and understand all or most of what you have read. Unless you know how, when, and what to read rapidly, you'll probably find you can't read all you should and want to read. In addition, you may be falling behind in your daily assignments, term papers, reports, etc.

SHOULD YOU READ EVERYTHING RAPIDLY?

Of course not. But neither should you read everything slowly. This is what a great many students tend to do. Your reading rate (number of words per minute you read) should be determined by what you are reading, why you are reading it, what you expect or are expected to get out of it. If you want to get just the general idea of a book or chapter, you will certainly read faster than if you were reading the same book or chapter critically, in depth, taking notes as you read, in preparation for a report or a term paper. You would read the daily newspaper faster than your chemistry textbook, a light humorous magazine article on suburban living faster than a serious, highly documented one on the population explosion or on the new African nations.

UNDERSTANDING COMES FIRST

Important as it is for you to learn to read rapidly, remember that you are reading primarily for understanding and for enjoyment. Rapid reading for its own sake doesn't make any sense whatever. It is what you understand of what you read that counts.

HOW TO READ RAPIDLY

Rapid reading is something you can learn to do easily and quickly, up to your speed and comprehension limit. You won't know what your limit is until you have tried to reach it. But too few of us do what we are capable of. You may discover that you can read only 400 or 500 words per minute comfortably and understandingly. That's fine. You're reading at your peak, not slogging along at 150 words per minute.

Here are some useful approaches to increasing your reading speed. Some of the suggestions you will be able to carry out on your own with your own books, magazines, newspapers. With others, you will need some expert help, especially for specific, daily practice materials.*

I. Before you open a book, know what you are reading for. Have a purpose. Adjust your reading speed to that purpose.

Looking for an author's date of birth? You don't have to read a whole biography or even a whole biographical sketch to get this. One quick look in an encyclopedia and you have what you want.

Reading a novel or short story for pleasure? You can breeze through it rapidly. You don't have to make a report on it. You don't have to take notes. You can just let yourself be carried along by the sheer movement of the plot. There is a legitimate place for this kind of comfortably rapid reading. If you don't or can't read like this, you'll be missing some very wonderful experiences.

Reading a serious poem? You'll have to slow down considerably to get its full flavor and meaning. Poetry presents special reading problems—rhythm, imagery, symbolic condensed language.

Reading a statistical report? Slow and easy does it here. You can't read factual, closely reasoned material rapidly. You shouldn't even try.

---

* We recommend that you buy one or both of these books. Their point of view, advice, and practice materials are just right.

Faster Reading Made Easy by Nila Blanton Smith (New York: Popular Library, 1963).
How to Read Faster and Better by Norman Lewis (New York: Thomas Y. Crowell, 1951).

Reading an essay? Here your reading rate would obviously depend on what you were reading the essay for.

To get the main idea: This you could do pretty quickly.

To get the author's ideas and point of view: This takes slower, closer reading. You need more time to mull over what you are reading. Here and there you will have to stop to reread just to be sure you have understood the author fully.

To write a critical report on the author's style: Even slower, more careful reading, with extra time out to take notes, underline significant passages, etc.

II. Use whatever leads the author gives you to get at the main ideas quickly: the introductions and summaries to books or chapters, the marginal headings and subheadings, etc.

III. Read for ideas. With your eyes, take in groups of words. Don't read single words. Word-by-word reading slows you down, clogs your understanding, and eventually confuses you.

IV. Pay special attention to the topic sentences of paragraphs. Most good writers get the main thought or idea into the topic sentence. Frequently the topic sentence leads off the paragraph. But this is not always so. You will sometimes find the topic sentence at or near the end of a paragraph.

V. Watch for transitional words, phrases, sentences. These tie one thought into another, and often tell you what to expect:

More of a similar nature: Further, furthermore, in addition, finally, moreover, next, first, second, third, also, another.

A conclusion or summary coming up: Hence, thus, therefore, for this reason, consequently.

A change in time or space: Meanwhile, at last, beneath, above, following, preceding, later, soon.

Specific illustrations or examples to follow: For example, in particular.

VI. Enlarge your vocabulary consciously, systematically. Don't leave anything to chance. Your vocabulary won't just grow by itself. You'll have to feed it and care for it regularly and intelligently. (See "How to Build a Vocabulary," page 64.) You won't ever be able to read rapidly if you are too frequently stopped in your tracks by words whose meanings you don't know or can't arrive at from the context.

VII. Practice some rapid reading every day. Do this either with prepared practice materials or with your own materials, preferably quite varied: newspaper, magazine, story, essay, etc. These practice sessions don't have to be long. But prepare for them carefully and be constantly aware of what you are trying to do. This may make you a bit self-conscious in the beginning, but this feeling will soon wear off.

VIII. Push yourself to read as fast as you can, but not to the point where you are reading only words and missing the meaning. Your aim here should be to get yourself to read at *your own maximum speed* and with *maximum understanding.* If you find you don't understand what you are reading, slow down. You're reading too fast.

Most readers are sluggish. They are capable of reading faster and more and better. By pushing yourself to your limit (depending, of course, on what you are reading and why), you will develop your skills and keep them trim, taut, flexible.

IX. When you read:

Don't move your head from side to side or up and down.

Don't say the words out loud or back in your throat with your mouth closed. This is called "vocalizing." It cuts your possible reading speed down to a walk. Let your eyes sweep over each line, taking in "thought units" rather than a word at a time. Eye-reading is easily ten times as fast and efficient as "vocalizing."

Don't look back over what you have read (unless, of course, you don't understand it at all). These "turnings-back" (called "regressions") tend to slow down your reading while at the same time they muddle your understanding. Keep your eyes and your mind moving ahead. If you are stumped by a word and can't figure out or guess at its meaning, underline it and come back to it when you have finished your reading. Only rarely does a single word stand between you and the meaning of a paragraph, chapter, or book. We suggest this technique only for developing speed in reading with practice materials. Naturally, when you are studying your daily assignments, you will have to handle the unfamiliar words quite differently.

Use a Reading Pacer if your school has one. This is an interesting and useful device. It consists of pages of reading matter and a shutter that exposes a set number of words per minute. You can control the speed of the shutter and thus the number of words per minute you can read and understand. You can start the pacer as low as you wish and then increase its speed as your reading speed improves. The pacer and other similar mechanical devices are not the answer to all your reading problems. But, if properly and intelligently used, they have proved very helpful.

CAREFUL READING

Much of your college reading will be close, critical, analytical, "between the lines," "in depth" reading. Your instructors will expect you to be able to probe deep and hard for basic facts, ideas, relationships. In this kind of searching, challenging reading you will be:

Understanding precisely and fully what an author is saying. Everything else that you do with what you read depends on how well and how completely you have understood basic ideas, characters, etc. This calls for alert, attentive reading for such things as the main idea, supporting details, facts, meaning of basic terms, answers to specific questions, etc.

Looking deeper into the author's motives, attitudes, etc., through what he says directly, through his style, his "tone," the kinds of words he applies to characters, situations, ideas, movements, the position he takes or doesn't take on issues.

Evaluating what you read by answering such questions as: Is this true? Does it make sense? Is it in accordance with the facts as I know them? Is the author a qualified authority? Does he present his point of view fairly and objectively? Or is he grinding an ax, indulging in special pleading, suppressing important facts, distorting others, presenting slanted or loaded statements? Is he making appeals to emotion and prejudice rather than reason?

Here are some simple things to keep in mind whenever you are doing any "careful reading":

Before you start, know exactly what you hope to get or are being asked to get out of your reading. Having a sharply defined purpose will give conscious direction to your reading and make you more alert to what you are reading for.

Give your full attention to what you are reading. You can't read carefully if only part of your mind is involved or if you are distracted by noise and interruptions.

Relax when you read. Try to put your problems aside. You can't solve them while you are reading. If you can't forget about your problems long enough to concentrate on what you are doing, you may need to talk with someone on campus— counselor, dean, rabbi, priest, minister, an older student—to help you solve your problems or cope with them well enough to keep them out of your way when you are working at a difficult assignment.

If you don't find everything you are looking for on the first reading, don't get worried. Worrying never helped anyone understand anything. It often can, and does, actually paralyze the worrier so he can't think straight at all. Read your assignment again, just as carefully as you did the first time. Keep a sharp eye out for what you seem to have missed. Since you have already found some of the answers you were looking for, you can, during this second reading, look more closely for what eluded you the first time.

Don't read too long at any one time. Careful reading is taxing and tiring. Stop after half to three-quarters of an hour. Look up from your book. Get up from your chair. Stretch your legs. Move around. Take a brief brisk walk. Think over what you have just read. Then, back to the mines. (See Chapter 8, How to Study.)

We hope we have made you aware of your reading needs and pointed out what you can do to improve your reading. But reading this chapter will not make you a better reader. This takes time and work, day in and day out. Reading improvement comes slowly. Don't expect any overnight miracles of yourself, your instructors, or your practice materials. Be patient. The rewards that will come to you will be well worth waiting and working for.

CHAPTER 7

WHAT TO READ

COLLEGE, as someone once observed, is a four-year reading course. Most of what you'll get out of college will
come from books. Of course, college is more than books. It's
the people you meet, the experiences you have, the way you
react to everything around you. But it is nonetheless true that
your basic ideas about yourself, your society, your fellow men,
life, literature, music, art, will come to you very largely from
books—and, naturally, from your teachers, who, in a sense, are
transmitting to you or helping you get at the essential message
of these books.

So—

The more you read
The more you like to read
The more intelligently you read
The more you retain of what you read
The more you'll get out of college.

It's as simple as all that!

When you get to college, your instructors will expect you to
be "a reader." They will expect that you will like books, that
all through high school you have read more than you have
been required to do, and that, therefore, you are ready to
meet the college's fairly stiff reading demands:

78

To read more books than you've ever had to read before—and
in less time

To read a variety of materials: textbooks, novels, drama, essays,
magazines, short stories, technical treatises, etc.

To read books and parts of books bearing on a single subject
or phase of a subject

To read difficult material critically, closely, and in depth

To read against a deadline—to complete your required reading on time, in time to take meaningful part in class discussions, and, yes, to pass the tests that are an inescapable part
of college.

Don't get any wrong notions about your college reading. It's
going to be interesting, challenging, eye-opening, and head-
opening. Some of it will move you as you have never before
been moved. Some of it will rock you intellectually, force you
to examine and re-examine most of your deeply cherished
ideals and convictions. Most of it you will enjoy. But all your
college reading will be harder and more demanding than your
high school reading.

Most college freshmen are overwhelmed by their reading
assignments. Quite understandably, for in high school they
never really prepared themselves for college:

► They never read enough books.
► They never read enough good, important books.
► They never read regularly, systematically, and intelligently.
► They never read on their own, purposefully and eagerly.

How about you? Are you ready for a college reading program? Not unless you've been doing lots of good, hard, steady,
wide reading all through high school. Certainly, if you haven't
read at least one good book a week from the time you entered
high school (a total of about two hundred and fifty solid, important books), the chances are that you will be starting your

college career with a handicap: not having read enough, not having acquired the reading habit.

A READING PROGRAM

Suppose you (like most college students) haven't read all you should have read. Is it too late for you to do anything about it? Not at all. If you haven't done all the reading you should have done, you can still do something to make up for at least part of the time you've lost. Will you be able to fill in all the gaps in your reading? Probably not. But you can make a considerable dent in that backlog of unread books by embarking right now on a manageable, sensible reading program that will give you the background, experiences, and habits you should have acquired long ago.

It won't be easy for you to do your current college reading and this "catch-up" reading at the same time. But if you're really serious about getting the most out of college, you won't mind the extra work. Actually, you're sure to find memorable moments of joy and excitement in the books you've missed so far.

Books, of course, are and must be the heart of your reading program. But you can't and won't be really well read unless you:

Read a good newspaper every day—one that covers the local, national, and international news fairly and completely. If your local newspaper doesn't meet these standards, supplement it with a good look at one of the large metropolitan newspapers which you should be able to consult in your local public library or in your college library.

Read a literary review. There is one in the Sunday issue of most newspapers. From it you will get some notion of what's doing in the exciting world of books.

Read a magazine of opinion that deals maturely and responsibly with today's important social and political ideas, problems, and personalities.

BOOKS YOU SHOULD HAVE READ

By the time you become a college freshman, you should have read all or most of the books on the list which follows. This is not by any means an exhaustive list. It certainly doesn't contain everyone's "favorites." In compiling this list we have drawn upon many sources and consulted many individuals. So we feel reasonably certain that there is wide, general agreement that this list includes the interesting, worthwhile books, the "great" books, the "classics," the "masterpieces," that should be part of every high school and college student's reading experiences.

Here are a few suggestions for using this list:

Check all the books that you have read. You will be pleased and encouraged to discover that you have already done part of your job. Knowing how much ground you have covered will make it easier for you to get on with the rest of your reading.

Check each book as you finish reading it. Why? To give you that special satisfaction that comes with getting something done that you've wanted to get done. This sense of achievement will sustain you when, occasionally and naturally, you may find the going rougher and less interesting than you had hoped.

Set up a reading schedule for yourself and stick to it. Plan to do *some* reading every day—no matter how much or how little (preferably *much*). But, in any event, read at least one nonassigned book a week during the regular college year, more than one if at all possible. Increase the number of books during the summer and other vacation periods. Remember that you'll need time to read other books that aren't on this list. The sooner you complete your "required" reading the more time you'll have to spend on current books, best-sellers, etc.

Fair warning! Some of these books won't catch your interest immediately. They were written in a fairly leisurely style. (You may be tempted to call it old-fashioned.) But don't put these books down if you aren't caught up in suspense, horror, sensationalism, plot complications in the first few pages or chapters. Don't get impatient. Give the author a chance to work his special magic on you as he has on countless readers before you.

If you just can't get even mildly interested in a book that has for generations held and moved readers like you, put it down. But come back to it again. You may be more receptive the second time around. Or you may be free of the distractions, problems, and tensions that kept you from getting involved in the book at the first reading.

You're lucky. You can buy practically all of the books on this list in low-cost paperback editions. For the first time in our history, a publishing revolution has made available to you the greatest books of all time for less per copy than the price of a movie. (If your local bookstore doesn't have these books in stock, consult a copy of *Paperback Books in Print* at your local library. This book lists every paperback published, with its price, and the address of the publisher.)

Buy as many of these books as you can. When you own a book, you can do important things with it and to it—things that will make it uniquely your own. You can mark up your own books lovingly and significantly. You can underline the words and passages that have a special meaning for you. You can argue with the author in the margins. You can comment on his style, his point of view, his handling of a character or an idea. And you can take your own sweet time reading a book you own. You can reread it and reread it until everything in it is yours.

If you've been "specializing" in mathematics, sciences, or foreign languages, these books will help you break out of the narrowness of taste and interest that all specialists ultimately fall into.

Aeschylus. *The Oresteia: Agamemnon, The Choëphoroe, The Eumenides*
Austen, Jane. *Pride and Prejudice*
Baldwin, James. *Nobody Knows My Name*
Balzac, Honoré de. *Père Goriot*
Barrie, James. *What Every Woman Knows*
Beebe, William. *Jungle Peace*
Bellamy, Edward. *Looking Backward*
Bennett, Arnold. *The Old Wives' Tale*
Brontë, Charlotte. *Jane Eyre*
Brontë, Emily. *Wuthering Heights*
Buck, Pearl S. *The Good Earth*
Bulfinch, Thomas. *The Age of Fable*
Bunyan, John. *The Pilgrim's Progress*
Butler, Samuel. *Erewhon*
———. *The Way of All Flesh*
Carroll, Lewis. *Alice in Wonderland*
———. *Through the Looking Glass*
Carson, Rachel. *The Sea Around Us*
Cather, Willa. *My Antonia*
———. *Death Comes for the Archbishop*
Cervantes, Miguel de. *Don Quixote*
Chaucer, Geoffrey. *The Canterbury Tales*
Chekhov, Anton. *Short Stories*
———. *The Cherry Orchard*
Clemens, Samuel L. (Mark Twain). *The Adventures of Tom Sawyer*
———. *The Adventures of Huckleberry Finn*
———. *Life on the Mississippi*
———. *A Connecticut Yankee in King Arthur's Court*
Coleridge, Samuel T. *The Rime of the Ancient Mariner*
Collins, Wilkie. *The Moonstone*

Conrad, Joseph. *Lord Jim*
————. *Typhoon*
————. *The Nigger of the "Narcissus"*
Cooper, James Fenimore. *The Last of the Mohicans*
Crane, Stephen. *The Red Badge of Courage*
Curie, Eve. *Madame Curie*
Day, Clarence. *Life with Father*
Defoe, Daniel. *Robinson Crusoe*
Dickens, Charles. *Great Expectations*
————. *David Copperfield*
————. *A Tale of Two Cities*
————. *The Pickwick Papers*
————. *Oliver Twist*
————. *A Christmas Carol*
Dickinson, Emily. *Poems*
Dostoievski, Feodor. *Crime and Punishment*
Doyle, Arthur Conan. *The Adventures of Sherlock Holmes*
Dumas, Alexandre. *The Three Musketeers*
————. *The Count of Monte Cristo*
Durant, Will. *The Story of Philosophy*
Eliot, George. *Silas Marner*
————. *The Mill on the Floss*
Emerson, Ralph Waldo. *Essays*
Euripides. *Medea, The Trojan Women, Electra*
Fitzgerald, F. Scott. *The Great Gatsby*
Flaubert, Gustave. *Madame Bovary*
Frank, Anne. *The Diary of a Young Girl*
Franklin, Benjamin. *Autobiography*
Galsworthy, John. *Justice*
————. *Loyalties*
————. *The Forsyte Saga*
Golding, William. *Lord of the Flies*
Goldsmith, Oliver. *The Vicar of Wakefield*
————. *She Stoops to Conquer*
Hamilton, Edith. *The Greek Way*
————. *The Roman Way*
Hawthorne, Nathaniel. *The Scarlet Letter*
————. *The House of the Seven Gables*
Hemingway, Ernest. *A Farewell to Arms*
————. *For Whom the Bell Tolls*

————. *The Old Man and the Sea*
Hersey, John. *Hiroshima*
Heyerdahl, Thor. *Kon-Tiki*
Homer. *The Iliad*
————. *The Odyssey*
Housman, A. E. *A Shropshire Lad*
Hudson, W. H. *Green Mansions*
Hugo, Victor. *Les Misérables*
————. *The Hunchback of Notre Dame*
Huxley, Aldous. *Brave New World*
Ibsen, Henrik. *A Doll's House*
————. *An Enemy of the People*
Irving, Washington. *The Sketch Book*
James, Henry. *The Turn of the Screw*
————. *The Portrait of a Lady*
Keats, John. *Poems*
Keller, Helen. *The Story of My Life*
Khayyam, Omar. *The Rubaiyat* (translated by Edward Fitzgerald)
Kipling, Rudyard. *Kim*
————. *Short Stories*
————. *Barrack Room Ballads and Other Poems*
Kruif, Paul de. *Microbe Hunters*
Lamb, Charles. *Essays of Elia*
Leacock, Stephen. *The Best of Leacock*
Lewis, Sinclair. *Babbitt*
————. *Arrowsmith*
————. *Main Street*
London, Jack. *The Call of the Wild*
————. *The Sea Wolf*
Malory, Sir Thomas. *Morte D'Arthur*
Mann, Thomas. *Buddenbrooks*
Marquand, John. *The Late George Apley*
Marquis, Don. *Archy and Mehitabel*
Masters, Edgar Lee. *A Spoon River Anthology*
Maugham, Somerset. *Of Human Bondage*
————. *The Moon and Sixpence*
Maupassant, Guy de. *Short Stories*
Melville, Herman. *Moby Dick*
Miller, Arthur. *Death of a Salesman*
Morley, Christopher. *The Haunted Bookshop*

————. *Parnassus on Wheels*
Munro, H. H. ("Saki"). *Short Stories of Saki*
Nash, Ogden. *Verse*
Nordhoff, Charles and Hall, J. N. *Mutiny on the "Bounty"*
————. *Men Against the Sea*
O'Hara, Mary. *My Friend Flicka*
O'Neill, Eugene. *Ah, Wilderness*
————. *The Emperor Jones*
Orwell, George. *Animal Farm*
————. *1984*
Paine, Thomas. *The Rights of Man*
Palgrave, Francis (ed.). *The Golden Treasury*
Paton, Alan. *Cry, the Beloved Country*
Plato. *The Dialogues*
Plutarch. *Lives of Noble Greeks and Romans*
Poe, Edgar Allan. *Poems*
————. *Tales*
Porter, W. S. (O. Henry). *Short Stories*
Remarque, Erich Maria. *All Quiet on the Western Front*
Robinson, James H. *The Mind in the Making*
Rolland, Romain. *Jean-Christophe*
Rolvaag, O. E. *Giants in the Earth*
Rostand, Edmond. *Cyrano de Bergerac*
Saint-Exupery, Antoine de. *Wind, Sand, and Stars*
Sandburg, Carl. *The People, Yes*
————. *Abraham Lincoln: The Prairie Years*
Saroyan, William. *The Human Comedy*
Scott, Walter. *Ivanhoe*
Shakespeare, William. *A Midsummer Night's Dream*
————. *As You Like It*
————. *Hamlet*
————. *Henry IV, Part I*
————. *Henry IV, Part II*
————. *Julius Caesar*
————. *King Lear*
————. *Macbeth*
————. *Othello*
————. *Richard III*
————. *Romeo and Juliet*
————. *The Merchant of Venice*

———. *The Tempest*
———. *Twelfth Night*
———. *The Sonnets*
Shaw, George Bernard. *Arms and the Man*
———. *Caesar and Cleopatra*
———. *Man and Superman*
———. *Pygmalion*
Sheridan, Richard B. *The Rivals*
Sophocles. *Antigone, Oedipus Rex, Oedipus at Colonus*
Steffens, Lincoln. *Autobiography*
Steinbeck, John. *The Red Pony and Other Stories*
———. *The Grapes of Wrath*
Stephens, James. *The Crock of Gold*
Stevenson, Robert L. *Treasure Island*
———. *Kidnapped*
———. *Dr. Jekyll and Mr. Hyde*
Stowe, Harriet Beecher. *Uncle Tom's Cabin*
Strachey, Lytton. *Eminent Victorians*
Swift, Jonathan. *Gulliver's Travels*
Synge, J. M. *The Playboy of the Western World*
———. *Riders to the Sea*
Tarkington, Booth. *Penrod*
———. *Alice Adams*
Thackeray, William M. *Vanity Fair*
Thoreau, Henry. *Walden*
Thurber, James. *A Thurber Carnival and Others*
Tolstoi, Leo. *Anna Karenina*
———. *War and Peace*
Turgenev, Ivan. *Fathers and Sons*
Untermeyer, Louis (ed.). *Modern American Poetry*
———. *Modern British Poetry*
Van Loon, Hendrik. *The Story of Mankind*
Verne, Jules. *Around the World in Eighty Days*
———. *20,000 Leagues under the Sea*
Washington, Booker T. *Up from Slavery*
Wells, H. G. *The Time Machine*
———. *The War of the Worlds*
———. *Outline of History*
Wharton, Edith. *Ethan Frome*
White, E. B. *One Man's Meat*

Whitman, Walt. *Leaves of Grass*
Wilde, Oscar. *The Picture of Dorian Gray*
————. *The Importance of Being Ernest*
Wilder, Thornton. *The Bridge of San Luis Rey*
————. *Our Town*
Williams, Oscar (ed.). *Immortal Poems of the English Language*
————. *A Little Treasury of Great Poetry*
————. *A Little Treasury of Modern Poetry*
Wolfe, Thomas. *Look Homeward, Angel*

We envy you reading the books on this list for the first time. The experiences and insights you will find in them will sharpen your awareness of the "human condition" and deepen your sympathy for and understanding of the common hopes and fulfillment we share.

CHAPTER 8

HOW TO STUDY

W HY do most students fail?
You're wrong. It is not because they don't have the
intelligence to understand what they're studying! And it is not
because their studies are too difficult for them! They fail because they don't know *how* to study or what study *means!* Add
to this number those who are on the edge of failure or in some
kind of academic trouble, and you have a virtual army of students handicapped by poor study habits and attitudes.

Shocking, isn't it? But it's true. What is even more distressing
is that most of this large-scale failure, near-failure, and unhappiness can be prevented. It isn't possible to keep every student from failing. But we know enough about authoritative,
useful, workable approaches to developing the best kind of
study habits to help most students fashion for themselves a successful academic career.

The following suggestions for effective study have been
drawn from the observations of experienced teachers and
counselors, and from the practices of successful students. Let
us be clear at the outset about one thing. These suggestions will
show you *how* to study more effectively. They won't make
what you have to learn any easier. They will, however, make
the learning of it pleasanter. You will learn more effectively
what you want to learn and must learn. But don't be deceived
into thinking that knowing *how* to study is the same as study-

ing. If you fall into this trap, you'll fail just as surely as the student who doesn't know how to study at all. As Lester Wittenberg points out in his excellent study manual,* "Students often fail because they know only that they want to succeed. They know what rewards they want, but they do not want to recognize that only work will get them these rewards. In short, students often fail because they are trying to get something for nothing."

WHAT IS STUDY?

► "Study is hard work," says William Armstrong.† "If you aren't working hard, the chances are you aren't really studying. . . . Education without sore muscles isn't worth much." There are no short cuts or easy roads in genuine study.

► Study is solitary work. Study is something that happens between you and your books. He studies best who studies alone.

► Good study habits last a lifetime. You may forget some of the things you've learned. But you won't forget *how* you learned them and *how* you studied to get them.

► You can learn how to study. No matter what kind of study habits you now have, you can make them better. Good students aren't born with a set of built-in good study habits. They make themselves into good students through persistent and intelligently planned study.

► Good study habits are the key to your success in school. The more effectively you study:

The more you get out of your work
The better your grades

* Lester Wittenberg, Jr., *A Study Manual* (Cambridge, Mass.: Educators Publishing Service).

† William Armstrong, *Study Is Hard Work* (New York: Harper and Brothers, 1956).

The better your chances are of getting into a graduate or professional school

The better your chances are of getting the job you want

The more prestige you enjoy among your classmates and
teachers

The easier and more relaxed you feel

The more you will enjoy college.

▶ Good study habits grow slowly and gradually. Improvement of your study habits comes slowly, too, as you eliminate
your old bad habits and replace them with new, good ones.
It takes time to develop your mind to the point where it can
do all the things a well-trained mind is expected to do:

Be at home in a number of areas—English, social studies,
physics, chemistry, mathematics, sociology, foreign languages

Move quickly and efficiently from French to calculus to English literature to biology in one evening—every evening

Memorize facts

Deal with scientific formulas

Grasp ideas

See relationships.

▶ It's easy to study what interests you. Much of what you are
required to study, however, may not attract you at first. The
best way to become interested in what doesn't interest you
is to study it. Sounds odd? But every successful student can
tell you how often his interest has been sparked when he really
got into his subjects. So don't wait for your interests to tell you
when or what you should study. You can acquire some interest
in most subjects by giving yourself a chance to get to know
them. Actually, says T. S. Eliot, "no one can become really
educated without having pursued some study in which he took
no interest . . . for it is a part of education to learn to interest
ourselves in subjects for which we have no aptitude."

The best kind of study takes place when:

You know why you are studying
You care about what you are studying
You approach your work feeling confident you can do it
You try to get the most out of your studies—not just enough
   to get by
You work for understanding, not just for grades.

THE BEST CONDITIONS FOR STUDY

There are perhaps some students who can make good on the boast, "I can study in a boiler factory." But unless you are extraordinary or eccentric, you will probably need somewhat more congenial and attractive conditions to study effectively.

An ample desk. A good minimum size would be about 30 by 18 inches. A flat-topped desk is preferable, with enough drawers to file and keep all your basic materials: pens, pencils, typing paper, carbons, folders, index cards, etc. Set your desk so that you do not face the campus or street when you are studying.

A small bookshelf next to or on your desk for the basic reference books you will be consulting frequently: dictionary, almanac, thesaurus, one-volume encyclopedia, grammar and usage manual, etc.

A simple chair. All of the votes are in favor of a simple, rugged, straight-backed chair with no cushions. You study best when you're not too comfortable or relaxed. A state of "mild tension" is just about right for the best results. For obvious reasons, avoid studying on a couch, easy chair, or in bed.

Good light. The light you use when you are studying should be bright and glare-free, and should generally come over your left shoulder onto whatever you are doing. Avoid having the light shine directly into your eyes. The entire room should have some light so that when you glance away from your book momentarily your eyes won't have to make too radical an adjustment.

Comfortable room temperature—not too hot or too cold.

A wall calendar. Preferably not too attractive or distracting. All you want it for is to act as a kind of "major strategy map" to enable you to block out your master schedule month by month, making note of holidays, special events, etc.

Wall decorations. By all means, dress up your room. You spend so much study time in it that it should be a place where you're comfortable and feel at home. You'll do well to avoid distracting pictures or illustrations. If you must have them around, however, place them where you won't be facing them when you study.

No external distractions. Turn off the radio and TV when you are ready to study. You can't study with either of these going, even "quietly." There are no quiet distractions. There's nothing whatever to the theory that you study better to the accompaniment of radio or TV. Reach an understanding with your family, friends, roommates, that you are not to be interrupted while you are studying. If the phone rings, you are out, unless it's an emergency. Have someone take the message for you. Call back when you are free.

Yes, it's that important for you not to be disturbed while you are studying. For if you answer the phone, you may literally drive out of your mind what it may have taken you half an hour to get fixed in your mind. When you resume your work, you may not be able to get back on the track again. Answering the telephone may easily nullify your whole evening's work.

Enlist the cooperation of everyone around you to respect your need for reasonable quiet while you are studying. Recognize, however, that you are not likely to get perfect quiet, or even what you would consider adequate quiet. You will have to learn how to study under conditions that fall a bit short of the ideal. Making this kind of adjustment is part of your education, too.

No internal distractions. We all have internal distractions: family worries, personal problems, worries about the present and the future. They are with us most of the time. When you sit down to study, however, you must be able to put these aside. If they persistently come to mind and actually keep you from studying, you may need professional help to alleviate your problems or to learn to cope with them so that, at least, you can lock them out of your mind while you're studying.

No bull sessions. Don't try to talk and study at the same time. You won't do either well. Your study is likely to suffer most. If you feel you must have a discussion with your family, friends, or roommates, get up from your desk, talk yourself out, and get back to your studies.

DOING THE ASSIGNMENT

There are many ways to skin a cat. And there are many ways to do an assignment. Not all ways of skinning a cat are correct or efficient. The same holds true for doing an assignment.

There is no one best method of doing an assignment. There are some very poor ones. We needn't discuss them here.

Here are some very good approaches to the assignment that have been tested and proved in practice. They have worked for thousands of students, and they should work for you, too.

Before you get down to doing the assignment, get an overview of what you are expected to do: the skills, facts, ideas you are expected to master, the ground you are expected to cover. You can get some notion of the scope and nature of the job before you by skimming the material, noting the chapter, section, and paragraph headings. You will find it useful, too, to try to relate what you have already learned to what you are going to do.

Have a specific goal or purpose in mind for each subject you are studying. Know what you want to achieve and approximately how much you'll be able to achieve in the time you've allotted for it. (See "The Study Schedule," pages 101-104.)

Warm up and get started quickly. Your mind is like a car on a cold day. It needs a warm-up period to get all its parts ready to operate smoothly and efficiently. You have to get yourself ready for study—free your mind of irrelevant matters that are cluttering it up at the moment, and shut off unpleasant, bothersome thoughts and problems. But don't take too long getting warmed up, or you'll go from head-scratching to nail-examining to pencil-chewing to dawdling to daydreaming —to no studying!

Study with a pencil in your hand so you can take notes. If you own the book, you can make notes and comments, raise questions in the margin. You can underline important points or passages. But be careful, or you'll soon find yourself underlining almost everything. Underline only what you would have put into your notebook if the book didn't belong to you.

As you cover a point or complete a section of your assignment, stop, take your eyes off the text and, in your mind, go over what you have covered. State it in your own words. Check with the text to see how accurately and fully you remember what you've read.

Cover your most difficult subjects first. Your mind is freshest and most receptive when you first start studying. At this point it will do its best with the toughest parts of your assignment. After an hour or two of wrestling with difficult subject matter, your mind, like your body, will begin to tire. It will still have plenty of energy left for easier subjects, but not quite enough for the more demanding ones.

Review and recheck your assignment as soon as you've

finished it. A substantial portion of what you learn has a distressing tendency to evaporate immediately after you've done your reading or studying. Just going over and over your work mechanically won't make it stick. Close your book. Cover the passage. Rephrase, restate, summarize the facts, ideas, and formulas in your own words without looking at the text. You must do this to fix what you have learned firmly in your mind.

After you've studied for about an hour, stop. Get up from your desk. Walk around a bit. Eat an apple, or a piece of candy if you don't have to watch calories. Do something different. This kind of brief change of pace is good for your muscles and your mind. Now you can go back to your studies.

Try to get all your assignments done before you go to bed. There's nothing like that "mission-accomplished" feeling for a good night's sleep.

Tomorrow's uncertainties are another good reason for clearing your desk at the end of the day. The time you planned to complete your unfinished business may be taken up by some event you couldn't possibly foresee. So you'll come to class unprepared and you won't fully understand what your teacher is talking about because it's all based on the assignment you thought you'd have time to finish before the class met—but something happened!

HOW TO MEMORIZE

You can't get very far in your studying without memorizing all kinds of things—dates, scientific formulas, events, names of men, books, characters in literature, etc. Memorize them you must, because memorizing them is the only way you can make them part of you.

Don't say, "I can't memorize." You can't *help* memorizing. You do it either well or poorly. Here's how to do it better:

Be sure you understand what you're trying to memorize.
The better you understand it, the more sense it will make and
the more likely it is to stick with you. It is possible to memorize
material that means little to you, but it's hardly worth the
effort. You'll forget it almost as soon as you've memorized it.

Your memory is like a muscle. It gets stronger and more
proficient the more you exercise it. The more you memorize,
the easier it becomes to memorize more.

Concentrate fully on what you're memorizing. Don't allow
anything to come between you and the content.

*Unless you have a phenomenal memory, you'll find that one
of the best ways to memorize anything is to go over it again
and again*—intelligently, of course, and knowing all along the
purpose and meaning of what you're trying to memorize.
Studies have shown that there is a very close relationship between how well and how much you remember of your assignments and how often you put your mind through the processes
of *meaningful repetition.*

*Don't try to memorize any long passages or substantial sets
of facts all at once.* Take them in easy bites. When you've finished with a passage or formula or concept, stop. Close your
book. In your mind's eye, go over the material. Check back
with the text to see how close you've come to restating the ex-
act substance and details of what you've learned. Do this at
various points throughout your study. After you've finished the
assignment, give it a grand review from beginning to end.

Just before class next day, go over your work again—first
without consulting the textbook. Jot down whatever you can
recall about last night's work. Then check it again with the
text. If you get a chance, discuss the lesson with some friends.
This is another way of reviewing and of strengthening your
memory.

Wherever you can, try to associate new materials—especially isolated facts like dates—with something else. This will give you an easy way of hooking the fact into your memory. It doesn't matter too much what device you use so long as it works for you.

You are no doubt familiar with the memory gimmick called a *mnemonic:*

> Thirty days hath September,
> April, June, and November.
> All the rest have thirty-one,
> Excepting February alone.
> Twenty-eight days is its store
> Till Leap Year gives it one day more.

It is certainly not great poetry, but it is one of the most effective mnemonics ever invented.

Remember the tune that helped you learn to spell Mississippi so you never forgot it? Mis-sis-sippi. It's a musical mnemonic, probably the most famous of all.

Some people memorize the correct spelling of *separate* because they see *a rat* in *separate*—or *secretary* because a *secretary* is someone who knows how to keep a *secret.*

Use the ready-made mnemonics if they work for you. But you'll need to invent your own to meet your special problems.

When you memorize, use as many of your senses as possible:

Sight. This is obvious, of course. You read the text. The words create images or ideas in your mind. Rereading the text and trying to memorize what you've read strengthens your visual memory.

Hearing. Not so obvious at first glance. But actually, you are employing your sense of hearing as a memory aid when you recite the main points of the lesson *aloud* to yourself, when you read a poem or a prose passage. What you are doing here simply is adding what the lesson *looks* like to what the lesson *sounds* like. You now have two of your senses working for you, helping you hold the lesson fast in your memory.

Touch. Can you *feel* a lesson? Not exactly—but almost. It's precisely what you are doing when you take notes or make a written summary or paraphrase of what you are reading. When you write out your ideas, you are, in a sense, putting them into some kind of shape that you can feel. As you give them this written form, you are reinforcing your senses of sight and hearing with your sense of touch.

By using as many of your senses as you can, you increase your chances of memorizing your work more completely.

Short, intensive periods of from fifteen to twenty minutes are best for memorizing material such as dates, verb forms or vocabulary in foreign languages, scientific and mathematical formulas. Fatigue is likely to set in if you try to extend these memory periods beyond the fifteen- or twenty-minute limit. For some unknown reason, most minds begin to lose their efficiency beyond this point. So if the work you must memorize will take you an hour to do, break it up into four fifteen-minute sections which you will tackle at various times during the day or evening.

You can safely and profitably increase the length of these memory periods when you're dealing with more meaningful, complex materials involving understanding of ideas and relationships in such subjects as social studies, science, English, and philosophy.

YOU MUST HAVE A SCHEDULE

A day is just twenty-four hours long—for the successful *and* the unsuccessful student. After deducting the time needed for sleeping, eating, relaxing, and play, both kinds of students have approximately the same number of hours for study.

The unsuccessful student knows better—but he chooses to

believe that time is elastic, that there are more hours in his day than in anyone else's day. So operating under this delusion, he rarely gets all his work done on time, if he gets it done at all.

The successful student knows he has just two things to work with—time and his abilities. He has been told, and he believes it, that time can be his slave or his master. With so much to learn and so little time to learn it, he has decided to make time work for him by developing and sticking to a schedule. This schedule, he has found:

Gives him a sense of power. Every day he knows where he is going, how far he has to go, and how long he has to make the journey. He knows, too, that he is calling the turn, that he is deciding what he is going to do, and when, and how much.

Increases his effectiveness as a student. He is getting the most out of every minute at his disposal. He doesn't waste any time deciding what to do next or wondering what he has left undone.

Keeps him free of worry and anxiety. He is no longer the victim of uncertainty and planlessness. He knows what he has to do. He has devised a workable plan for getting it done. And he has time to rest and play and have fun, too.

Develops in him the capacity to work efficiently and regularly. Systematic study becomes useful and pleasant. Following a sensible, daily, meaningful routine every day makes it progressively easier for the student to study and to deploy his limited time and energies with maximum effectiveness. Because he knows what he wants to do and has worked out a plan for getting it done well and on time, he can spend all his time studying instead of, like the unsuccessful student, just getting ready to study or wondering what to study first.

If you are wise, you will take a leaf from the successful student's book and make a study schedule.

THE STUDY SCHEDULE

Just a word of caution: making out a study schedule is the easiest part of your job. Almost anybody can construct a satisfactory study schedule. The true test of your character as a student is how faithfully you stick to your schedule. The schedule is the road map for your trip. It isn't the trip itself.

As you work out your schedule, here are some things to consider:

Block out the hours at which you must meet all your fixed responsibilities—the "musts" in your life. These include your classes, mealtimes, sleep, etc. Here you have comparatively little choice.

Schedule your study periods at times when you know you work best: morning, evening, before meals, etc. You may not always be able to follow this part of your schedule completely. An important test, an exceptionally difficult assignment, or some kind of emergency may throw you off schedule occasionally. Accept the unexpected as a natural part of life. Start to become worried when the unexpected interruptions of your schedule become frequent or habitual.

Allow ample study time for each subject. Set aside about two hours for each hour you spend in class.

Plan to study the same subjects at the same time each day. At first blush, this may seem a bit mechanical to you. But experience has shown that it is less so than it sounds. Actually, it helps you develop a rhythm and pattern of study so that when you sit down to study you will fall into it naturally and easily.

Make provision in your daily and weekly scheduling for reports, papers, research projects, readings, etc. Here you will be doing some of your most important long-range planning. Since these assignments are due at different times during the semester, you will have to estimate approximately how long each will take you to complete.

Estimate approximately how much time you have between the date the project is announced and the due date.

Plan your work on each project so that it doesn't interfere with your daily assignments.

Stagger your work on each project so that you don't suddenly find yourself with several incomplete reports on your hands, a few important tests in some subjects, plus the usual run of daily assignments. This happens to great numbers of students. It needn't happen to you if you think about what you have to do and set aside the time in which to do it.

Pace your studies to avoid too much last-minute studying and "cramming." You can do this by setting aside definite daily or weekly review periods in your schedule.

Keep your schedule balanced and varied. All work and no play make Jack a rather dull, incomplete human being, and a less effective student, too. You are more than a walking mind. You have a body that needs exercise just as much as your mind does. You have a need for friends and social activities. Walking, visiting a museum, going to a concert are also essential parts of your daily life. Make room for these experiences in your schedule. And don't forget to allow some time (not too much) for that best, simplest, and most invigorating of all pleasures—doing nothing—by yourself or with a boon companion.

Make your schedule tight enough for you to complete all your required work. But leave some slack in it so that you are able to deviate from it occasionally to meet emergencies or special demands as they arise.

Go through your first schedule, regarding it as something in the nature of a trial run. Try to do everything as you have planned, but watch carefully those points at which the schedule doesn't seem to work out according to plan.

SAMPLE STUDY SCHEDULE

	SUN.	MON.	TUES.	WED.	THURS.	FRI.	SAT.
7:00		Breakfast. Morning walk. Read newspaper. Listen to news or morning musicale.					
8:00		Review last night's work or do some advance studying. Walk to class. Talk with friends.					
9:00	Chapel	English	French	English	French	English	French
10:00		Study hist.	Study chem.	Study French	Study math.		Library
11:00		Math.	History	Math.	History	Math.	History
12:00	Lunch						
1:00		Chem. lecture	Study chem.	Chem. lecture	Study math.		Reading
2:00	Weekly review	Study Eng.	Study math.	Study French	Phys. Ed.	Team	Prep. for papers and projects
3:00		Study math.	Chem. Lab.	Study hist.			
4:00	Recreation sports, etc.	Study math.		Study hist.	Study Eng.		
5:00				Library			
6:00	Dinner						
7:00	Study Eng.	Study French	Study Eng.	Meeting			Recreation
8:00		Study hist.	Study French	Movie	Glee Club	Reading	
9:00	Study math.	Study hist.	Study math.	Study French	Study Eng.		Dates, etc.
10:00	Shower. Relax. Radio, TV, book, magazine. Bed.						

You are, at this stage, bound to make some errors in estimating your own abilities, the difficulty of your courses, the time it takes you to cover your work, the number and nature of distractions you encounter, and their effect on you. You may, for example, discover that you need less time for chemistry than you had planned. But your mathematics has taken more than its allotted time. You will have time left over from your chemistry allotment to give to your mathematics.

By the end of the first week, you'll be able to gauge with some accuracy approximately how much time to give to each of your subjects. Your second week's schedule will, of course, reflect these changed estimates.

Make your schedule out at least a week ahead, and try to have it ready before the week starts. So—when Monday rolls around, you'll know how the whole week shapes up for you. Knowing this will give orderly direction to your activities. Some students work on a day-to-day schedule. They make up their Tuesday schedule on Monday. We don't recommend this —unless, of course, you enjoy living from hand to mouth and can do it efficiently. Successful students agree that you can't work well with anything less than a weekly schedule.

HOW TO STUDY SPECIFIC SUBJECTS

The basic study techniques we have been discussing will apply to all of your subjects. There are, however, special study problems in each of the major subject matter areas. The study of foreign languages, for example, calls for much more sheer memory work than philosophy or English literature. In mastering a foreign language, you must not only acquire a new vocabulary, but you must, in addition, learn to listen to the language very carefully so you can come to speak it with some accuracy and fluency. In foreign language study, obviously, you will be engaging in more oral reading and speaking activities than, let us say, in mathematics or chemistry. Reading a poem intelligently calls for skills somewhat different from those required for reading a science or history text.

Ask your teachers to list for you the study techniques they think you need to master their specific subjects most effectively. Be sure to make it clear that you don't want general study helps, but specific advice and suggestions for dealing with the problems inherent in and characteristic of the subject. Your teacher can find nothing but pleasure and gratification in your search for the best way to get the most out of your studies.

CHAPTER 9
HOW TO TAKE NOTES

A SIGNIFICANT part of what you will learn in college will come to you through lectures. Here you will get the special flavor of your teachers' personalities, their enthusiasm for and their special approach to their subjects, the wisdom of their research, and their unique faculty for organizing and presenting material.

To understand lectures, you'll have to learn how to listen. Learn how to listen? Haven't you been listening all your life to your parents, your friends, your teachers, your minister, priest, or rabbi, the radio, TV? Of course you have. But you haven't always been *hearing* what you've been listening to— or you have been listening with one ear, giving only part of your attention to the speaker, part to something else, your own thoughts or something around you. Tests have proved that while people spend about three times as much time listening as they spend reading, they remember only about half of what they hear!

If you listen to college lectures the way you've been listening generally, you'll be in trouble. Listening to lectures is different from any other kind of listening you've had to do because:

► You have no control over the kind of lecturer you will get. He may be inspiring or dull. He may speak too rapidly or too slowly. His presentation may be crystal-clear and easy to un-

106

derstand, or muddy and obscure. No matter. Your job is to follow him, listen to him, make sense and order out of what you are hearing. Not all lecturers are perfect. But their imperfections won't be accepted as an excuse for your failure to understand the lecture and get its highlights into your notes.

► You have to listen attentively no matter how you happen to be feeling at the moment. You won't be able to hear this lecture again. You'll have to get it when it is being said, no matter how it is being said.

► The lecture room is full of distractions. If you let them distract you, a picture on the wall, a pleasant outdoor scene, the rustling of papers, the talkative friends around you, some especially attractive boy or girl you'd like to meet or have met may keep you from hearing or understanding what the lecturer is saying.

HOW TO LISTEN

Does it now follow that the perfect professor and the completely attentive, undistracted student make up the perfect lecture? Not at all. A lecture is as good as what you get out of it. The perfect presentation and the absence of internal and external distractions are merely the setting for the lecture. What comes out of this setting depends almost entirely on the listener—how intelligently he listens and what he does with what he hears.

You didn't come into this world prepared to listen to lectures. This is something you have to learn: *how to listen*. The sooner and the better you learn how to listen, the more you'll get out of college. Listening is a complicated skill. But as with every other skill, you become more adept at it with constant, intelligent practice.

"To listen well," says Roger Garrison in *The Adventure of*

*Learning in College,** "is first to respond creatively with your-self. This requires at least as much energy from you as talking; real attention is not passive." It is a "steady, silent, inner con-versation with the lecturer."

Real listening requires active response. Even though you can't talk back to the lecturer, you must respond to and be in-volved in what he is saying. If you don't, you are acting like a sponge, merely soaking up what you hear. And sponges don't learn. Here are some of the things you will have to learn how to do if you want to become a "good listener":

Come prepared to listen, to react, to respond. If your pro-fessor is uninteresting and undemanding, don't make his fail-ures an excuse for not keeping your mind working. True, the lecturer should demand sustained, intellectual effort of you. But if he doesn't, demand it of yourself. Make a conscious ef-fort to become interested, and you will find that you are really interested, in spite of your professor's inadequacies.

Listen intently, purposefully, thoughtfully. Concentrate on *what* the speaker is saying. Don't spend your time resenting his personality or delivery or approach to the subject. Ideally, every lecturer should keep you on the edge of your seat, intel-lectually stimulated and excited every moment. But it doesn't happen this way. Poor lecturers, however, frequently have challenging, important things to say. That's what you are after. So keep your mind tuned for what's important—the substance, not the manner.

Don't reject too quickly ideas you don't like or haven't met before. Keep your mind open so that you can understand fully what the lecturer is trying to say, the context in which he is developing his ideas. Be aware of your prejudices and strong feelings. They will prevent you from fully understanding a point of view different from your own. Examine every idea

* Harper and Brothers, New York City, 1959.

thoroughly and objectively. If you finally decide to reject it, you will at least have thought through your position. You will not have acted hastily or blindly. You will have been doing what every thinking person should do:

Understanding an idea
Challenging it if it needs challenging
Turning it over in your mind, looking at it from every angle
Accepting it completely, with good reason, or rejecting it completely with good reason, or accepting or rejecting it in part, with good reason.

All this responding, thinking, analyzing, accepting, rejecting will be almost useless to you unless you get it down in some intelligible form. This is what your lecture notes are for—to capture and preserve for you the substance of the lectures, together with your own questions and thoughts about what you have been hearing and absorbing.

Most high school students and many college students don't know how to take notes because they have never been taught how. They haven't learned the simplest note-taking techniques. They try to record everything the lecturer is saying. But all too often they are left at the end of the lecture with either a very inadequate summary or a set of confused, disconnected jottings that in a few days become practically unintelligible.

There is no one sure-fire note-taking method that will enable you to get down everything the lecturer says and everything you are thinking about while he is lecturing. But there are some well-tested principles and devices that will guide and improve your own note-taking.

Whatever method of note-taking you use will be made easier if you can take a one-year shorthand course or a concentrated summer session or private school course. If you don't have the time to devote to one of the older shorthand systems, try your hand at an ABC system like Speedwriting. A six weeks course will meet your note-taking needs. If you can't manage to master any formal shorthand system, develop your own by abbreviating words, using symbols, etc.

NOTE-TAKING TECHNIQUES

First, a few "bread and butter" matters:

Take your notes on a good-sized sheet. The standard 8½ by 11 will do for most purposes.

For obvious reasons, keep your lecture notes in a sturdy, looseleaf folder. Thus you'll be able to shift your notes around, add to them, remove them for filing, insert material you may have missed.

Put the course number or name, the date, and a page number on each sheet. This will enable you to keep your notes together in some kind of order.

Take your notes in ink, or in pencil that won't smudge. You will want to refer to them again and again. They won't be of much use to you if they aren't readable.

Write legibly and neatly. You'll have to make a special effort to do this because you will be under pressure throughout the lecture, listening critically, evaluating what you hear, recording what you think is important, making your private marginal notations, etc.

Divide each sheet into two parts by drawing a line down the middle. Use the left-hand portion for recording what the lecturer says; the right-hand portion for your comments, questions, recommended readings, notes or reminders to yourself— all related to, growing out of, or suggested by the lecture.

When you miss a lecture, borrow a classmate's notes.

Now for the real essence of note-taking:

Don't try to get down everything the lecturer says. Unless you are a shorthand expert, you won't succeed. Besides, everything the lecturer says may not be worth recording. If you are intent on getting everything down, you won't be able to distinguish between what is important and what is not, either while you are taking notes or when you review your notes and try to make some sense and order out of them.

Keep your mind on the main points the lecturer is making. Underline these points in your notes. Add supporting details, reasons. Try to state the lecturer's ideas in your own words. This is the best kind of note-taking. But, under pressure, you won't always be able to do this, so when you can't, take down the lecturer's own words. Be sure, however, that you know exactly what the lecturer's original words mean before you set them down.

Try to get an orderly view of the sequence and development of the lecturer's ideas. With some lectures, you won't have any difficulty whatever. They have good, logical, well-organized minds, so their presentations move smoothly and clearly from point to point. Frequently, such lecturers will even tell you what major points they are trying to establish and what conclusions they hope to arrive at. During the lecture they will stop when they have made a point, to underscore it and to help you fix it more firmly in your mind. Such lecturers realize how difficult it is to listen critically and attentively and at the same time take meaningful notes.

Most lecturers, however, are not so well organized, not so sympathetically aware of the needs and limitations of their young listeners. They believe that you should be able to get the point of any lecture by yourself without any special assistance from the lecturer. But you can discover what this kind of lecturer thinks is important by noting:

The amount of time he spends on a particular point. The more important he thinks it is, the more time and attention he is likely to give to it.

The number of times he makes the same point. This is generally a very good indicator of the importance the lecturer attaches to it.

His gestures, the tone of his voice. By observing these carefully, you will soon learn to tell when the lecturer is dwelling on an important point. His gestures are likely to become more forceful, more animated. He will be trying to "hammer home" his point. His voice, too, will betray his added concern for something he wants to be sure you won't miss or mistake. In his speech, which may grow noticeably more rapid or more deliberate or more dramatic, you will be able to detect a more urgent, more insistent note. This will tell you that the lecturer wants you to pay special attention to what he is saying.

If the lecture isn't well-organized, don't try to organize it while you are following it and taking notes. Put down everything as it comes to you. Leave out as little as possible. Note in the right-hand column of your notes what you think is superfluous, trivial, not related to the lecture. (Lecturers often wander from the point.) After the lecture you can set things in order.

As the lecture proceeds, note questions which the lecturer has not answered about things you don't understand. You can look them up later or discuss them with your instructor or classmates. The more questions you pose the more likely you are to be actively involved in what the lecturer is saying.

Relate what you hear to what you already know. Tie every bit of new information you get into the fabric of your knowledge.

Note especially in the right-hand column of your notes:

New materials or points of view you had not hitherto encountered or that are not covered in your textbook

Clarification and explanation of matters that you had not understood until now

Apt quotations, illustrations, comments, anecdotes, etc.

Books, articles, authors which the lecturer suggests that you look into on your own. These very often prove more exciting and stimulating than the original lecture by giving you fresh insights and opening up new fields for you to venture into.

Review your notes, recast them where necessary, underline main points, as soon after class as possible. While the lecture is still fresh in your mind, you can give the notes the form they should have. At some time each evening meet with a few of your classmates to compare notes and to discuss the main points made in the day's lectures. But be careful not to let these meetings turn into general bull sessions.

CHAPTER 10

THE TERM PAPER

SOMETIME during your freshman year (usually in the first semester), you will probably be required, in at least one of your courses, to write a "paper"—variously called a term paper, a library paper, a research paper, a source paper, a reference paper. This is a fairly standard assignment in most colleges. As you proceed through college, you will be writing more papers, more extensive and more demanding ones.

What is the reason for a term paper? Does writing a term paper achieve purposes important enough to make it a "must" for every college student? The overwhelming majority of colleges think so. They feel that planning, preparing, and writing a paper gives you valuable practice and experience in:

Choosing and limiting a subject so that you can handle it effectively within the time and with the available facilities

Using library techniques and resources to find precisely the information you are looking for

Reading for a specific purpose

Selecting out of what you read those materials—and only those —that make a significant, meaningful contribution to your paper

Taking selective notes on your reading

Weaving your notes into your paper

Outlining the scope of your paper

And, last, but by no means least, exercising, developing, and refining your writing skills and your vocabulary.

Writing a paper, in short, introduces you to the basic disciplines of scholarly thought and research and prepares you to deal with the challenges of advanced work in college, graduate school, and beyond.

WHAT A TERM PAPER IS NOT

It is not an original, learned thesis or dissertation. It does not call for very extended research over long periods of time, nor does it demand that you produce or discover something so new and startling that it will make the mature scholars in the field sit up and take notice.

It is not just a rewording or paraphrasing of what you have read.

It is not a summary, however complete, of one or two references or authorities you have consulted.

WHAT A TERM PAPER IS

Individual instructors set their own standards and requirements for papers. But they are pretty much agreed that a good paper:

Has a point of view

Is carefully chosen and limited

Is logically planned and developed

Is appropriately documented with quotations and references to books, magazines, and other source materials

Draws upon a variety of source materials selected for their specific bearing on the topic

Supports its statements, assumptions, and conclusions with pertinent, authoritative data and evidence

Is simply and clearly written
Is free of errors in grammar, punctuation, usage, etc.

CHOOSING THE TOPIC

This sounds easy, doesn't it? Yes, if you just choose the first topic that comes to your mind. That's a nice, quick, simple way. But it is not likely to prove the best way. If you give it the thought it deserves, choosing a topic is, in many ways, one of the most difficult, and certainly one of the most important, decisions you must make in writing a term paper.

The following suggestions should help you choose your topic intelligently. They are based on the experiences of students who have tried them successfully, and of instructors who know from first-hand observation what the common pitfalls are and how they can best be avoided.

Know exactly what kind of paper you are expected to write, how long it should be, when it is due. Listen carefully to your instructor as he explains the nature of the paper, its scope, its limits. If you are not absolutely clear on every point, see your instructor before you even start planning your paper. There is at least one student in every college class who, when he gets an F on his paper for not doing as he was told, whines, "I didn't know we were expected to . . . I thought that . . ." The instructor is properly unmoved. The F stands. Moral: Don't try to guess what is in your instructor's mind. Ask him.

Some instructors invite their students to confer with them, to help them choose their topics, give them constructive leads to follow, suggest ways of limiting the topic, etc. You are lucky if you have this kind of instructor. Don't ignore his invitation. But before you come to the conference, jot down any questions and problems you have about the writing of your paper. Don't be concerned at this point with small details, such as the kind of typing paper to use, width of margins, form for the bibliography. These can be settled later. Right now your prime target is choosing a topic which you will be able to handle successfully.

Choose a topic that interests you—one you know something about or have had some experience with. You will generally do your best work with a topic that has some special meaning for you, that you'd like to learn more about. Anyone, from the world's great psychologists to the kids around the corner trying to perfect their mumblety-peg technique, can tell you that there is nothing like *interest* to involve and sustain your energies for any length of time. The longer the period you must spend on a specific job, the more important it is that you be deeply interested in what you are doing and in how it will come out.

What if you're not vitally interested in any of the topics your instructor suggests, or if you can't find one that strikes a real spark? Pick one that interests you mildly or even slightly. Do some preliminary reading in and around the topic. You may discover something that will fan your interest or pique your curiosity.

Sometimes, try as you will, you can't find a topic that attracts you. What then? You'll just have to do your best with a topic that doesn't interest you very much. You'll have to work harder at this kind of topic than at one you are naturally drawn to. But remember that you will be judged, not by what interests you, but by what kind of paper you ultimately produce. Your instructor won't take "I wasn't interested, sir," as an excuse for a poor performance. Here, as elsewhere in and after college, a mark of your maturity will be your ability to do superbly well things you don't like or aren't deeply interested in.

Choose a subject on which your local and/or college library has plenty of easily available materials. Distinguish here between what is available in the whole field and what is available in your library. You'll have to work with what your library has. Before you finally decide on your topic, make sure that you can get everything or almost everything you will need in your library. There's no point in choosing a good, interesting topic if your library doesn't have all or most of the important references you will have to consult. A quick check with the card catalog, the periodical indexes, and the encyclopedias should net you all the information you need at this point. If you don't think you'll have enough materials to work with, consult the librarian. He may be able to supplement your meager findings. If he can't, switch your topic to one that your library's resources can cope with.

You can avoid running into this problem by staying away from topics on which very little has been written, topics that are wholly speculative, limited, or obscure.

Don't disparage your library because it doesn't have exactly what you need for your immediate special purposes. Very few libraries are equipped to handle all the needs of all students.

Choose a topic that will make it possible for you to use a variety of sources: books, magazines, general and special encyclopedias, etc. (see Chapter 5, How to Use the Library). The more kinds of materials you use, the more skillful you'll become in handling the basic tools of scholarship. Avoid topics that are thinly covered by one or two books or a few magazine articles. Here again your preliminary research will tell you what kinds of sources are available to you.

Avoid subjects that call for technical information you do not have or cannot understand because you do not have the necessary background or experience. Obvious, isn't it? Yet paradoxically many students embark upon projects in which they are certain to encounter concepts and relationships that they will not be able to grasp. They are attracted to a topic they would like to know more about. But their previous training and education have not prepared them to deal with what they find. So, after doing some hard digging, they are forced to abandon that topic and start searching for one they should have chosen in the first place, one which their training, education, and reading would make them feel at home with.

Don't make the mistake of thinking that a term paper is designed to take the place of a basic course or to give you an understanding of subjects or areas you are not yet ready to enter. In writing the term paper you are, through the use of the tools of research, extending, deepening, refining, adding to, building on what you already know.

Choose a topic that is not too narrow, limited, or special. Offhand, you would think that the smaller the area you are working in, the easier it will be for you. Not true at all. You could, for example, do much better with a topic like "The Eye of the Bee" than with "Eye Diseases in the Bee," simply because more has been written on "The Eye of the Bee" than on "Eye Diseases in the Bee." Again, a quick look at available materials in your library will tell you whether your topic is worth pursuing.

Avoid too broad, too ambitious topics. A term paper is not expected to be the definitive work in the field. It is just a simple, modest exercise utilizing certain fundamental scholarly tools and disciplines. Keep this in mind, too. The term paper is not supposed to occupy all your time. It is only part of a large variety of experiences called college. The term paper has a deadline on it. You have only a limited period in which to complete it, and many things to do in the process of completing it. So don't rush into a topic that you won't be able to read your way through and around in the time you have. Don't, for example, start working on "The Essay." You'll never find your way out of this topic. Stake out an area that you can reasonably cover, such as "The Essays of William Hazlitt"—still fairly demanding, but possible. Or try "The Early Essays of William

Hazlitt" or "Hazlitt's Essays on Shakespeare." Now you've cut the topic down to a size you can handle and still come up with a fairly respectable, interesting paper.

Avoid vague, general subjects like "Insurance Companies" or "Politics." You can't do much with these until you have decided how you want to deal with them, what particular phase you're interested in exploring. Certainly you shouldn't start doing any reading or note-taking on such topics until you have reduced them to meaningful, manageable size. You may, of course, keep the *title* of your paper vague, but be sure that the focus on your subject is unmistakably sharp and clear.

Choose a subject that you will find worth looking into—if possible one that is related to the courses you are taking. Thus, writing your paper will develop your skills as a beginning researcher and scholar, and add something substantial and significant to your knowledge of the subject.

Avoid topics that are too controversial. This does not mean that you should confine yourself to safe, colorless topics. Your mind will never grow if you simply stick to the settled issues, the solved problems. We make this suggestion about *too* controversial topics simply to alert you to what may happen if you do get involved in such topics. You won't be able to handle them within the time you have to devote to a term paper. Once you plunge into emotion-charged areas, you will inevitably find yourself "taking sides," giving only one side (your side) of the controversy, failing to state the opposition's point of view fairly or adequately. When you do this (and you'll find it hard to avoid), you are well on the way to writing an unbalanced paper.

Just to be sure you don't misunderstand, let's say it again. Avoid only the *too* controversial topics. Don't avoid topics about which there are or are likely to be differences of opinion. Your paper doesn't have to be pale and neutral to be acceptable.

Controversy will add color and spice to your thinking and writing. But deep and violent controversies will generally make it difficult for you to write the kind of logically developed, balanced, thoroughly documented paper your instructor will expect of you.

NEXT STEPS

Once you've selected and limited your topic and done enough preliminary research to assure yourself that you will have adequate, varied materials to consult, you are ready to get down to the actual job of doing the paper. This involves a number of steps:

Making a rough outline of how you plan to develop your topic. Without this you'll be lost. You may change or even discard this outline as you get deeper into your subject, but you must have something to start with which will give some form and direction to your reading and research.

Collecting and evaluating materials that have some bearing on your topic.

Taking full, accurate, pertinent, usable, readable notes on your reading. Every one of these words is important: *full, accurate, pertinent, usable, readable* notes.

Arranging your notes so that you can "spot" them where they belong in your paper—to support a point you are making; to add a colorful quotation, etc.

Actually writing and revising the paper.

Inserting footnotes and adding a bibliography.

Each of the steps we have outlined has a specific set of techniques and disciplines all its own. Space does not permit us to spell them out in detail here. Fortunately there are now available a number of very inexpensive, useful handbooks dealing with all the specific technical problems you will encounter in doing a paper.* You can probably consult them in your library or buy them in your college bookstore or order them directly from the publishers. We urge you to buy some of them if you possibly can. Familiarize yourself with these books *before* you are assigned your first paper. This will take part or all of the shock out of your instructor's announcement that you will be required to hand in three papers during the term, the first one due in four weeks! To students who have never written a paper, who don't know where or how to start or where to get information on where and how to start, this can be a most disturbing experience.

Having studied one of these handbooks beforehand won't solve all your problems, but it will surely give you a calm, sensible, orderly approach to the writing of your paper. Your instructor may recommend other "how-to" books or give you a list of similar suggestions that he or the department wants you to follow. In either event, you won't have that terribly lost and frantic feeling that comes over so many students when they first encounter the term paper.

* The following handbooks all contain "model" term papers which you are sure to find worth examining. Your paper naturally won't be just like any of these model papers, but seeing how they follow the rules for writing good term papers should enlighten and encourage you.

Student's Guide for Writing College Papers by Kate L. Turabian (Chicago: University of Chicago Press), $1.25.
Writing Term Papers and Reports by George Shelton Hubbell (New York: Barnes & Noble), $1.25.
The Term Paper—Step by Step by Gilbert Kahn and Donald J. D. Mulkerne (Garden City, N. Y.: Doubleday & Company), $1.00.
The Research Paper by Lucyle Hook and Mary Virginia Gaver (Englewood Cliffs, N. J.: Prentice-Hall).

CHAPTER 11

HOW TO TAKE A TEST

YOU and your fellow students belong to the most tested generation our society has ever known. From the moment you were able to make marks on paper, you have been tested. As you progressed through grade school into high school and college, you were subjected to more and more tests. Actually, you have been tested for something by somebody practically every day you've spent in school.

If you have been intelligent about all this testing, you have accepted it calmly and philosophically, at times wondering why it was necessary, what it all proved, why at this late date someone hadn't been able to come up with a simpler and better way of appraising your accomplishments, strengths, and weaknesses. You have listened patiently to those who favor testing—and more of it. And you have lent a sympathetic ear to those who think all tests should be abolished—together with the testers. But you realize, as Benjamin Franklin did, that in this world nothing is certain, except death and taxes. And if he were alive today, he would surely have added, "and tests."

You were tested before you got into college to determine whether you are fit for college, and for which college. In college, there will be many more tests. So, obviously, the sensible thing to do is to learn how to take tests successfully. Yes, you *can* learn how to take a test, just as you can learn chemistry, literature, foreign languages, swimming, dancing, ice-skating.

Some few students take tests with no apparent stress or strain. To most students, however, a test is an ordeal that they never seem quite ready for, no matter how often they face it. They do poorly on tests chiefly because they frighten themselves into a state of paralysis before and during tests. Others fail tests or don't do as well as they should, because:

▶ They don't know how to budget their test time. They don't finish, often leaving important, heavily weighted questions unanswered, because they never got to them, or worse still, never even read these questions or noticed how many credits were attached to them.
▶ They don't do what the question asks them to do!
▶ They do what they aren't asked to do!
▶ They leave out questions!

Year in and year out, thousands of unwary, unhappy students are trapped by their own anxiety, ignorance, and carelessness. And it's all so unnecessary. For we now know why students do poorly on tests. We know, too, what they can do to improve their scores and their test-taking techniques. These simple techniques won't guarantee you a perfect grade. But they will make it possible for you to do your best every time you take a test, to answer every question fully and as intelligently as you can.

WHAT IS THE BEST PREPARATION FOR A TEST?

Study. Study. Study. Good, hard, conscientious study— every day in every subject. You start preparing for your tests the first day you enter class. Everything you hear in class, every recitation you take part in, all the notes you take, every book you read and discuss, is in a very real sense preparation for your tests. Of course, learning is more than preparing for and taking tests. But you can learn all you have to learn and still be prepared for the inevitable test. There's no conflict here at all. Don't confine your learning activities to those things that you *think* may appear on a test. In this kind of guessing game you will almost invariably lose. Your chances of predicting the questions that will appear on a test are fantastically slim. More important, however, in trying to do this you won't be learning all that you should be learning, because you'll be so busy trying to decide what will or won't appear on the test! You can avoid this futile and destructive pastime by studying every day as if you were taking your tests tomorrow.

Don't fall into this all-too-common practice: "I can't give much time to this assignment now. I'll review it intensively just before the test." Don't kid yourself. *You can't review something you haven't learned!* Review time is not for learning anything new. It's for "re-viewing" (taking another look at) what you have learned. True, it's never too late to learn. You can, at this time, master what you failed to master earlier. But while you are doing this, you aren't *reviewing* anything. You are neglecting large areas of material that you should be brushing up on if you expect to do your best on the upcoming examinations. You can't *not study,* and then expect to use your review time for study, and still have time left for review. You just don't have that much time.

And while we're on the subject of what not to do, let us strongly urge you to:

Avoid last-minute cramming.

Avoid all-night coffee, cigarette, cold-towel sessions; "pep" or tranquilizing pills.

These are probably the two worst ways to prepare for a test. We know that they are widely prescribed and widely followed—but only by those who don't know any better or whose failure to plan their lives intelligently drives them to these pointless and unprofitable activities.

APPROACHING THE TEST

The way you are feeling when you take a test and the way you feel about the test can affect your performance. If you're not in good physical condition and if your attitude toward the test is wrong, it doesn't matter how well you know your subject matter. You won't be able to do your best. So:

Keep physically fit. Exercise regularly. Eat sensibly. Get enough sleep. Then you'll be able to stand up to any test. Make no mistake: taking a test, particularly when a lot depends on your grade, can be an exhausting physical experience. It's not unlike running a mile or two. If you're in good physical shape you can stand the examination gaff. Your mind will work better if your body is functioning soundly. Though the old Romans weren't plagued by tests, they knew a thing or two about how the mind and body work together. You could do worse than follow the Roman prescription for success: *Mens sana in corpore sano* (a sound mind in a sound body).

Keep emotionally fit. More than anything else, your feelings about the test—before and during—determine how much of what you know you can set down on paper. You find this hard to believe? Then think back for a moment to those friends of yours who "black out" or "clam up" when they take a test. What happens to them? They are literally paralyzed by their own feelings of fear and anxiety.

Come into the test room feeling you're going to pass—maybe not as high as you would like to, but pass. You're not just whistling in the dark when you do this. Most students pass most of their tests. If you have done your studying and reviewing effectively, if you have been getting passing or near-passing grades all semester, you can reasonably expect to come through the test in one piece. Thinking this way will at least put you into the proper frame of mind for taking the test.

Don't fight the test. Don't look upon it as part of a conspiracy to deprive you of your constitutional freedoms. Regard it simply as one of life's necessary burdens that you share with the rest of us. Feel superior to the test if you like, but don't relax your guard. Do all the test asks you to do. Do it well. That's much better than allowing it to get you so riled up you can't think or write straight.

Don't try to dream up questions you think may appear on the test. The chances are a thousand to one against your being able to do this anyhow. So why torture yourself?

Don't spend any time just before a test trying to discover how much you don't know, how much ground you haven't covered. It's too late now to do anything about it. You have covered the ground or you haven't covered it. Besides, since the test questions don't even pretend to touch every phase of the semester's work, they will very likely deal with material that your professor feels any student should be expected to know. Very few, if any, instructors try to "catch" students. They look upon tests as an opportunity for you to demonstrate how much you know, how well you understand the basic facts, and how well you can apply the basic ideas you have learned.

Don't try to figure out how much better than you your brighter friends will do. They probably will do better than you because they're brighter—and maybe because they have studied harder. You can't possibly get any benefit at this point from comparing yourself with such friends, but you can get yourself mildly depressed thinking about things you aren't responsible for and can't change—your native abilities and your friends.

Don't come into the examination pitying yourself. You may have had a rougher time than most people you know. Perhaps you have been too tired, too worried, too harassed by financial and other problems to give your all to your studies. Perhaps your roommates have interfered with your studying. Perhaps your instructor wasn't as good as your friends' instructors. Perhaps, perhaps, perhaps . . . Your paper will be graded for what you are able to put into it. You won't get a single credit for any of your personal problems, no matter how deep and acute they may be. Someone on campus (doctor, dean, counselor) may be able to help you with these problems. But don't let your feelings about yourself distract you during the test. Concentrate on the test, not on yourself.

REVIEWING FOR A TEST

Before taking a test you will of course want to review the work you'll be tested on. You'd be silly not to. It's quite normal to forget part of what you have learned, to get a bit hazy about facts, ideas, trends, relationships. Intelligent review warms up your mind, brings to the surface things you may have forgotten, brightens and strengthens your original insights and understandings, prepares you to face the test with the confidence that comes from knowing that you know.

There are many ways of reviewing for a test. Here are some simple suggestions that successful students follow:

Before you start your review, look over everything you have covered to date. Check your textbooks, lecture notes, etc.

Examine the ground that you have covered so far to determine:

Which materials you thoroughly understand (these will require little review—just a once-over lightly at most).

Which materials you are a little uncertain about (more attention to these, of course).

Which materials you just didn't understand the first time

around. These, naturally, will get most of your time and attention. It may even be necessary for you to ask one of your abler fellow students to give you some help. This is nothing to be ashamed of. It's done in the best of colleges and by the best students. It's unintelligent not to ask for help when you need it.

The essential point in reviewing is to concentrate your limited time in the areas where you are weakest.

Leave ample time for review—at least a week before your tests. Don't try last-minute, night-before, "crash" reviews. These rarely work well. Most frequently they leave you tense and exhausted just at the time (before a test) when you should be relaxed and rested.

Estimate the number of hours per day you will need for review. You can't do this precisely, but you can come fairly close.

Draw up a review schedule, and stick to it. Establish a priority list that will take into account:

Which subjects come first in your test schedule—these, obviously, you will have to review first.
Which areas require most attention.

Keep this in mind, too. You won't be able to give all your time to review. While you are preparing for your tests, you are still going to classes (except during finals) and you must keep up with your daily assignments. It's not easy to follow a "review" schedule and a "study" schedule at the same time. But you can do it, as hundreds of thousands of successful students have done. It requires only planning your activities and budgeting your time. (See Chapter 8, How to Study.)

TAKING THE TEST

The night before the test, relax—just relax. Don't do any studying. Take a walk. See a good movie, or watch TV. Read a book that has nothing to do with anything you've studied. What's the point of all this? Simply to keep your mind free of anything that will prevent your getting the good night's rest you'll need for tomorrow's test.

Get up early—early enough to have a leisurely, substantial breakfast and arrive at the examination room with time to spare. Don't underestimate the importance of being ahead of time. Nothing will more surely handicap you on the examination than that flustered, anxious, breathless, just-made-it arrival. Remember, if you are a commuting student, that, for reasons we all know, trains and buses don't always run on schedule. Allow time for delays and tie-ups.

Bring your watch. You'll need it to allocate the proper amount of time for each question. The examination room may not have a clock. You won't be allowed to consult a classmate's watch.

Read the questions and test directions—carefully, slowly. Don't start to answer any question until you know *exactly* what you are expected to do. Pretty obvious, isn't it? Yet a shockingly large number of students fail test after test because they don't read the questions *carefully* and *slowly*.

Don't dawdle. Don't examine your fingernails. Don't suck your pen. Don't look out the window. Concentrate on the test, not on yourself or your feelings. Every test is, in a sense, a time test. You need every minute to get what you know down on paper. You will be judged by how much you can say and how pertinently and well you say it.

Budget your time. Allocate a fair portion of the total test time to each question (see pages 132-135). Check frequently throughout the test to see that you are keeping to your time schedule. You may have to revise it as you go along. But at least you'll know when you're giving too much or too little time to individual questions.

Pay no attention to what your classmates are doing or how they look while they are taking the test. They can do you no good whatever during the test. But they can, by their looks and actions, distract you and add to your anxiety. Don't be impressed by the student who completes his test while you are only halfway through. He may very well have given up. Or he may be one of the brilliant ones who breeze through every test. At any rate, he isn't you, and you don't really know how well he answered the questions. So don't try to measure your success or failure by what you *think* he may have done.

Don't panic if your mind goes blank on a specific question or part of a question. At one time or another, this happens to most students. Sit tight and calmly think your way through or around whatever it is that has suddenly stopped you in your tracks. Generally, you'll find that in some magical, unexplainable way, you'll start thinking and writing again. Don't get panicky. This is the surest way to stop all thought processes. If, after a few minutes, you can't seem to get on with your answer, just drop it. Go on to another question. Later, come back to the point where you were stumped. Usually you'll find that you are able to think your problem through without any special difficulty.

KINDS OF TESTS

The tests you have taken and will take fall roughly into two categories.

Essay Tests. The questions in essay tests make the heaviest demands on students. Teachers and students agree that essay questions are harder to handle effectively than any other kind of test question. These tests try to measure:

How much you know

How skillfully you can select from what you know the facts and ideas that bear upon the question

How well you can organize your ideas and how clearly you can express them.

Objective Tests. These tests try to measure much the same qualities and achievements that the essay-type test measures, but with one very important difference. The objective-type test question doesn't require you to get your ideas down in writing. A simple check mark does the trick. Of course, it's really not so simple. You can't make that check mark intelligently unless you have studied the questions carefully. Your choice is based on a very complicated set of mental operations. Even checking the wrong answer requires some thought!

The most familiar types of objective-type questions are true-false, matching, completion, and multiple-choice. You have probably handled all of these in standardized reading and mental abilities tests.

ANSWERING THE ESSAY TEST

Go through the whole test quickly. Put a check mark next to the questions you think you'll have no trouble answering. Put a question mark next to the questions you aren't sure of or are likely to have some difficulty with.

Note how many credits are allotted to each question. Divide your time so that the question carrying the most credit gets the most attention. This may sound a bit mechanical, but it makes good sense. Generally speaking, the higher the credit value your instructor has set on a question, the more time he expects you to give to it. The credit he allocates to questions is your professor's way of pointing out their relative value.

Roughly, this is how you should calculate the time you plan to give to specific questions. Suppose, for example, that you are taking a two-hour examination. The total number of points for all questions is 100. A 25-credit question then would get one-fourth of the examination time, or thirty minutes. You may not need all this time. Fine. Then you'll have extra time for the questions that may prove difficult and may require more time than you have set aside for them.

Answer the easy questions first. You'll probably be able to answer these in less time than you plan. This will give you something of an emotional edge when you tackle the tougher ones—and it will leave you proportionately more time for them.

Read the instructions carefully. Don't start answering a question until you are absolutely certain you know what you are expected to do. Underline key words like *compare, contrast, describe, analyze, list, discuss.* Be sure you know what they mean. You can't answer the question intelligently unless you do.

Think and plan before you write. Organize your answer. Use any kind of outline system you like, but set down briefly and concisely the major points and minor points you are going to develop. Indicate briefly the facts, details, reasons, figures you intend to use to support any position you take. While you are planning your answer, jot down any ideas that come to you that are in any way related to the question. You may finally decide not to use them, but at least have them down where you can see them and decide how and where you can fit them into your answer. Pay particular attention to the *major points.* Be sure to cover these before you go on to the *minor points.* Your grade will depend, of course, on how well you cover *all* points, major and minor. Don't skip the minor points, but bear this in mind: the major points are naturally given greater weight and more credit. When you have completed your answer, reread it to see whether you have covered all the points listed in your outline.

Work on one question at a time. That's all anyone can do well—one thing at a time. Don't worry about that third question that you put a question mark next to and that you think may give you some trouble when you get to it. Don't imagine or anticipate troubles. You'll have enough to do to deal with them when you come to them.

Answer the questions as fully as you can in the time you allot to them. Get down what you know as simply and as completely as you can. Don't overwrite. Don't belabor an idea. Don't try to be exhaustive or definitive. No one expects you to be.

Check each question as you answer it just to be doubly sure you don't omit one. On every test, there is always some student who fails, or gets a lower grade than he should have, simply because he didn't keep track of the questions he had answered and those he still had to answer. Don't let this happen to you.

After you have answered all the questions, reread your paper. Check each answer against your outline. Keep a sharp eye out for errors of fact, omissions of parts of answers, unclear statements, errors in usage, spelling, etc.

ANSWERING THE OBJECTIVE-TYPE TEST

Read through the whole test quickly. Put a check mark next to the questions you think you'll have no trouble answering. Put a question mark next to the questions you aren't sure of or are likely to have some difficulty with.

Calculate the approximate time you have for each question by dividing the number of questions into the total test time.

Test time: 2 hours = 120 minutes
Number of questions: 60
Time per question: 2 minutes.

Of course, it won't work out just like this. You'll probably be spending less than two minutes on some questions, more on others. But doing this bit of arithmetic before you start the test will give you a rough notion about how to divide your time.

Read the test instructions carefully. Do as you are told. Argue after the test if you feel like it, but not before or during.

Answer the easy questions first.

Don't spend too much time on any one question. If you can't get at the answer in a reasonable time, go on to the next question.

Find out what the penalty is for wrong answers. If there is no *extra* penalty for wrong answers, guess—but only at those answers you feel at least fairly sure of. Don't engage in blind, aimless guessing.

Underline key words like "only," "always," "may," "most," etc. These words tell you whether there are exceptions to the statement. *"Only," "always"* mean that there are no exceptions. *"May"* and *"most"* mean that there are some exceptions.

Read all choices in multiple-choice questions. Eliminate the obviously wrong answers. Choose carefully between the remaining answers. One of these is the right answer, not necessarily the perfect answer, but closer to it than the others.

When you finish your paper, take all the time you can to check your answers, particularly those you had to struggle with and had doubts about.

Don't expect to get a perfect score. Hardly anybody does on a well-constructed multiple-choice test. That's how these tests are designed—with questions ranging from the fairly simple to the extremely difficult. So, if some questions stump you, don't jump to the conclusion that you will fail the test or make a poor showing. Go right on to the questions you can answer. You can safely assume that, no matter what standards your professor applies, you will do as well as most and better than some of your classmates.

CHAPTER 12

THE UPPERCLASS YEARS

YOU are now a sophomore. You have successfully passed the academic requirements of your freshman year. It wasn't easy. Freshman year rarely is. But you made it and, in so doing, you showed enough maturity and self-discipline to use your new freedom in college intelligently and constructively. You're on your way.

Now you are ready to face the challenges of your sophomore, junior, and senior years. Each of these years, of course, will present special and somewhat different problems for you, but in each year you will meet the same basic problem that you met and mastered in freshman year—planning your life so that you give full and proper attention to your studies, your friends, your family, your cultural, athletic and social interests, your present needs and future plans.

SOPHOMORE YEAR

"SOPHOMORE SLUMP"

There is one problem so universal and so characteristic of sophomore year that it has been given a special name—"sophomore slump." Many, many students each year fall victims to this slump. Some recover without serious aftereffects. Others just slump out of college.

137

What causes sophomore slump? What can students do to avoid this slump? To get out of it quickly?

Here are some of the things that tend to disturb and un-balance sophomores and together, or individually, can produce Sophomore Slump.

Overconfidence. Many sophomores in reviewing the re-sults of their first year are satisfied with their accomplishments. The work was not quite so difficult as they expected and, though their marks could have been better, they were not bad for a start. In those first nine months they learned how to sepa-rate the essential from the unessential in readings and lectures. They now know how to take notes, how to manage their time, how to read and study, etc. They have gathered from the class ahead complete scouting reports on sophomore teachers and they know what will be expected from them in each course. They are confident they can pass all their courses. In fact, they are overconfident but, alas, don't know it.

Overconfident sophomores are tempted to cut more classes than freshmen, certain that their friends' or roommates' notes will fill in any gaps. They won't. But the cocky sophomores aren't going to find this out until after the first test. They post-pone the reading that isn't due for three weeks, forgetting that during the last two days of the reading assignment library books are often very difficult to get, since their equally over-confident and procrastinating classmates will be fighting for the same books. They generally don't get the books for the first assignment.

Does this worry them? Very little. Again, they rely on their friends who did the reading and took notes. They promise themselves that next time they will start on their weekly read-ing assignments earlier. They probably won't.

They flunk the first test. This upsets them a bit, but they calm themselves and regain their overconfidence with thoughts that this is only the first test and not even a big one. They can make up everything on the next test.

They continue to kid themselves. Having gotten 40 on the first test without preparing, they figure they can get 90 on the second test with a little studying. Averaging 40 and 90 they now have 65. Sounds plausible. But it rarely works out this way. In addition, that first failure has led their teachers to suspect that they are lazy or incompetent. How are they going to upgrade their teachers' estimate of their work?

In every type of human endeavor, overconfidence is a great destroyer. Sophomores are no exception.

Too many activities. Yes, we agree that "All work and no play makes Jack a dull boy." We know, too, that much education takes place outside classrooms and laboratories. You need leisure time to allow your thoughts to settle. You need some activity to give you a change of pace, to add zest to your intellectual endeavors. This is precisely what extracurricular activities at your college are designed to do for you, and they will do it and do it well if you take them in moderation and give them their proper place in your schedule.

During the first semester of sophomore year in many colleges leaders of activities are looking for new blood. Organizations like the student newspapers, bands, orchestras, singing groups, fraternities, sororities, civil rights groups, etc., hold try-outs for sophomores.

You intentionally and intelligently remained out of most activities the first year. You wanted to get off to a good start in your studies, and you did. Now you want to make a place for yourself on the campus. You want to show everyone you have leadership qualities. Recruiters from the campus organizations have told you how important it is to "be somebody." Your fraternity or sorority leaders have impressed you with the position of your group on campus and how much your Brothers or

Sisters count on your contributions to the "house." Your father and others have suggested that you may find it easier to get jobs after college if you have some extracurricular achievements to your credit.

So you scramble around trying to fit yourself into this activity or that, not always because you believe in the activity or really want to spend time in it, but because you feel you have to be one of the gang. While you are busy being one of the gang, you slight your studies, you put second things first. If we seem to belittle all activities, remember we are discussing them here as one of the causes of sophomore slump. (For more on these activities, see Chapter 3, Freshman Year, page 35.)

Loss of purpose. Sometime during their college careers, many students suddenly seem to lose their sense of purpose and their desire to learn. They become moody, restless, and indifferent. Sophomores are more susceptible to this state of mind than most upperclassmen. It may last a week, a month, or even a semester. It generally brings with it lowered or even failing marks and sometimes academic suspension or probation. Students who have been through these periods of apathy and indifference have identified some of the factors that tend to produce them.

Before you came to college your world and your sense of values had a kind of logical, sensible, and satisfying order. At least they made sense to you. Now your ideals and values have been shaken. You are not quite so sure what is true or false, good or bad. Maybe the shock of contrary ideas and ideals came from classmates, maybe from a course or a teacher. It matters little, for all you know is that everything that used to be so clear to you now seems a bit fuzzy.

These feelings of doubt, wonder, and perplexity are the feelings all young men and women have when they first leave their homes and neighborhoods, whether they go to college, to the Armed Forces, or to work. At eighteen, most students are operating under an acquired or inherited faith or set of values. You can borrow the family umbrella and get protection from the rain, but you can't always borrow your parents' faith and ideals and expect them to make your life safe and pleasant. You are an individual living in a certain time and place and your greatest lifetime challenge is that of developing a philosophy of your own, a set of controlling ideas that suit you. Doubt is an anvil on which you hammer out the new faith.

Be slow to discard the faith of your fathers and mothers, the customs of your own home and community, for these were developed over a long period of time and after much experience. It may help you to remember that you are not alone in your struggles to find your new self. Since time began, youth has had difficulty finding and traveling the road to maturity and understanding.

Perhaps your faith in college and education has been shaken by your experience of your first year and a half. You probably came to college thinking that all courses would be exciting and all teaching inspiring. Now you know much learning is not exciting, but just plain, lonely, hard work. Furthermore, you think you had better teachers in high school, or at least so it seems now. You expected much more of college. Now you are keenly disappointed. Why bother, you ask yourself? No one seems to care or to be interested in you or even in education itself.

You think that nothing you are studying seems to have any relationship to a job or career or to the immediate world around you. You can't see how the study of classical civilization, eighteenth-century poetry, or philosophy will help you get a job or keep one. Nothing you are studying seems to be practical or useful.

The wrong program. Sophomore year is likely to be the time when your first suspicions that you might be in the wrong program or curriculum seem to be confirmed. You may, for example, have elected a pre-medical program, not because of any great passionate interest in medicine, but because your father wanted you to be a doctor or your grandfather said it was the noblest profession of all. You went along to please them. Being a doctor, you thought, might not be so bad. But failing marks in organic chemistry and physics have given you some strong reasons to cast about for another career. For the moment at least you don't know where you are heading. This can be very upsetting, especially since only the other day you were sure you wanted to be a doctor.

Perhaps you are a girl taking a home economics or a classics program. Now you discover, after a year or more of work, that you are not interested in what you thought you might want to take as a major. You are at loose ends.

Unusual circumstances. Students do not always slide slowly into sophomore slump. Sometimes they are suddenly and unexpectedly plummeted into it by such things as:

An unfavorable change in family finances, which forces a student to wonder what will happen to him and his family and makes him feel guilty about staying in college.
The unexpected death of a close relative or friend.
A summer or a vacation love affair. Back at school the student finds it hard to concentrate with the loved one so far away.
Home problems—illness, divorce, brother or sister in trouble.
An accident that hospitalizes a student for months, or an illness that lingers on for some time.

We wish we could tell you that there is one easy, certain method of shaking off sophomore slump, regardless of its cause. But there is no universal remedy. Your Freshman Dean, your teachers, your counselors all have had experience with students in the throes of sophomore slump. They, more than anyone else, can help you examine your own individual situation and problems and can suggest to you solutions that have helped other students in the past. Do not hesitate to enlist their aid and support when you see the first symptoms of sophomore slump.

CURRICULUM CHECK

Early in sophomore year, review your college's curricular requirements for moving into junior and senior year, for course distribution, especially for majors or honors work, and for the requirements for graduation. Registrars are usually the watchdogs in these matters, but don't depend entirely on them. Keep close check on yourself and see your adviser or the registrar if you are not clear about any of these matters.

Do you, for instance, have the required scholastic average, grade-point average, units, or credits to take the courses you want to take next semester and in the next two years? What grades will you need in sophomore year to qualify for a major, honors work, or for whatever special programs your college may offer in the last two years? Early in your sophomore year, check your plans for all future work. Then check again in the spring of sophomore year for your final program.

TO TRANSFER OR NOT TO TRANSFER

In Chapter 3 we pointed out why freshmen frequently want to transfer to other institutions. Thoughts about transfer may arise in sophomore year, too, and for at least two legitimate reasons:

(1) You may be in a large university where most of the courses you want are lecture courses, where you can't easily talk to your instructors because they assign their graduate-student assistants to work with undergraduates. You may have difficulty spending extra time in laboratory research because priority on laboratory equipment is given to graduate students, leaving less laboratory time for undergraduates like you.

(2) You may be in a small college which does not offer the range and depth of material you need in the area you have selected for your upperclass concentration. For instance, your summer projects or your outside reading may have given you a desire to concentrate on studies of the Far East or Africa, and your college may have too few or no courses in these fields. Or you may find it impossible to take a dual major in mathematics and biology.

If you have a B average, which many colleges expect from transferees, discuss your problems with your teachers and counselors, who will gladly help you transfer if they can't make arrangements for you to follow your interests in your present college. They may help you locate the kind of curriculum you want at other colleges.

Read the catalogs of other colleges carefully. Visit them if you can during Christmas vacation or at other vacation periods. Talk to students who attend these colleges. Don't transfer unless and until you are positive that the college you plan to transfer to has everything or almost everything you aren't getting now.

JUNIOR YEAR ABROAD

The question of whether you want to take your junior year abroad will have to be settled in your sophomore year. The beginning of this year is the time to make a careful study of the programs offered abroad and particularly of your college's attitude toward this kind of education.

At present there are more than one hundred institutions offering their own programs for the junior year abroad. In addition, many colleges which do not have such programs cooperate in and recognize the programs directed by other institutions. You don't have to attend a particular college to participate in its junior year abroad program.

Junior year abroad is attractive for various reasons:

▶ It is one of the best ways to learn the language and culture of another country.

▶ It is romantically exciting to spend a year in Rome, Paris, Berlin, or some other European city.

▶ It usually costs no more than the regular year at the college one is attending.

▶ Students who feel they are in a rut in their present college think that a change of scenery will get them out of it. They hope this year abroad will give them a renewed zest and interest in their work.

▶ Some students feel that this may be their only chance to go abroad.

▶ A girl friend or boy friend who is in another college and can be seen only during vacation is going abroad, so why not make the same trip for nine months in Paris or London?

It has been our experience that students who have spent their junior year abroad have often wasted their time because they have done it for the wrong reasons. True, they have had a wonderful *social* year. They have met a variety of people. They have learned to have fun without any hard work, and they can speak the language well enough to put on a slight display in the presence of a native of "their" country. But they have not done anything serious with their minds. They have learned very little about the country where they were staying. They have not come back with a new desire to add to their knowledge of its language, culture, politics, art, music, or the problems of its people.

We would urge you to move slowly in considering a year abroad. Think instead of a summer abroad. There are an increasing number of summer programs for students of language and culture. In this way you will not break the continuity of your education or the force of your concentration in your chosen field—a concentration which should start in earnest in junior year. Before you do anything about a year abroad, read a study entitled *Undergraduate Study Abroad*, by Stephen Freeman, published in the summer of 1964 by the Institute for International Education, 809 United Nations Plaza, New York City, New York. This book presents objectively the dangers and rewards of your year abroad. Your library probably has a copy.

JUNIOR YEAR

Junior year is the time to focus a major portion of your attention on the area that is of special interest to you. You are now free of the distribution requirements in your curriculum. You can begin the groundwork for your major, your senior honors thesis, or your final concentrated research project. You can choose courses you are really concerned with.

In addition to the subjects in which you plan to concentrate, consider courses in subjects you will probably never be able to study again in a formal way. If your concentration is in mathematics and science and you have taken only required courses in other fields, this is the year to take a course or two in English, literature, philosophy, art, music, or some other subject that will make your life more meaningful and more interesting.

If you have time, try auditing a course. When you audit a course, you attend the lectures and do the reading, but have the happy privilege of skipping tests. You do not have to write papers, either, but this is an opportunity which you should accept, for as a rule it is only through writing that you learn to clarify your thinking on any subject.

Now is the time to begin to consolidate your postcollege plans, to investigate more thoroughly the reading material in your college library and placement office, and to talk to visitors who come to the campus to discuss careers and various occupations. This is the year to sharpen your vocational thinking. (See Chapter 14, After College, What?)

If graduate school is your next goal, talk to the individual in the administration who counsels students about graduate schools, fellowships, application procedures, etc. Many applications for fellowships, graduate schools, etc., must be presented early in the fall of senior year. So do some preliminary thinking now. Decide what studies you want to pursue and where you can get the best preparation and training.

TRANSFER STUDENTS

If you have entered a four-year college at the junior level as a transfer student, you have special problems, particularly if you come from a community college or junior college. These problems will center around the proper choice of a curriculum, adjustment to new academic demands, and fitting yourself into a new society where groups are already pretty well formed, some of which will welcome you and some of which will hold you at a distance for a while.

Concentrate your efforts on your academic work; that is where they will count most. Too many transferees try too hard to be accepted immediately by established groups. Resist this natural desire. Be content to form new friendships slowly. Enter into the regular class and out-of-class activities by small, easy steps. In time you will make a comfortable place for yourself if you let things develop naturally as you go about your daily work.

SENIOR YEAR

It doesn't seem possible that you are now a senior. Those first three years seem to have gone much faster than you expected. And now you are not quite sure whether you want this last year to hurry or stand still.

We hope that you have found an area of concentration into which you can throw yourself with some excitement and interest. We hope, too, that the writing of your major paper or the production of your honors thesis or your senior research will be the most rewarding intellectual experience you've had. It should be.

Early in the year you will have to decide whether you want to go to graduate school. If you do, you must file your application early, and complete your plans for interviews when these are required, either at the graduate schools of your choice or on your own campus if graduate schools send representatives to your college.

Your marks, your scores on the Graduate Record Examinations (get information about these from the dean's office), your deans' and instructors' recommendations, and your activities will all be part of the record you will present to graduate schools. These do not of course tell the full story about your growth, development, and achievements. So take this opportunity to look back over your college years and to write a report on yourself which will point up any of your achievements that will not be officially listed or that cannot be measured by test scores or marks. You may, for example, have had a job during your college days that contributed to your well-being, not only financially, but in teaching you more about how to work with people, how to meet time demands, and how to take direction. You may have served your community in some capacity which doesn't reveal itself in your transcript. You may have worked with the Boys' Club, Boy Scouts, Girl Scouts, or for some local civic or social organization. Get letters of reference from people with whom you have worked. See that these letters become part of your record and are sent to the schools of your choice. Sincere, meaningful letters of commendation from your teachers, counselors, deans, as well as outsiders who know you well, carry weight with admissions committees.

If you are considering a career in business, work closely with the placement office to get leads and to see that your records are complete and up to date. You will also want to take every opportunity to be interviewed by visiting personnel men who will be coming to your college in search of promising, able young people.

If you are a man and have not done your military service between high school and college and are in a college which doesn't have an R.O.T.C. program, you will, of course, have to consider the possibilities for service in the Armed Forces. Most colleges have an adviser on military service. Talk to him about the various kinds of opportunities open to graduating college students. Since military conditions and opportunities are constantly changing, get the latest information from recruiting officers who visit the campus or who operate in areas near your home or college.

If you are a girl taking a general education or liberal arts program, learn shorthand and typing in your senior year if you haven't acquired these skills earlier. You may be able to get a job as a clerk at the ribbon counter in a department store without any previous business training. But more interesting and better-paying starting jobs are more likely to be available to you if you have some proficiency in shorthand and typing.

Many colleges require comprehensive examinations in the major field of your concentration at the end of senior year. Far too many students put off the necessary review work until late in the year. Don't fall into this trap. Plan a systematic approach to the review of material covered in your major field and start it no later than Christmas vacation. The tendency in such reviews is to try to learn too much about too many things. Concentrate on the key figures, ideas, trends, and events in your major subject. Try to see relationships between the work covered in your first two years and your last two. (See Chapter 11, How to Take a Test.)

We hope very much that your college experience will bring you a heightened curiosity about the world around you and some knowledge of how to approach the many problems that will arise out of your daily life. We hope college will be, for you, the beginning of a lifetime of learning, research, and discovery.

CHAPTER 13
YOU'RE OUT!

I T WON'T happen to me," you said, when you first discovered that half (about 500,000) of the boys and girls who entered college with you would not graduate on schedule, and that some would never get a degree. But now, in spite of all the good advice you've received, it *has* happened to you. You have become a college drop-out.

You don't like the sound of that word "drop-out," do you? Neither do we. We don't like what it has come to stand for, either. Most people look upon drop-outs as students who have failed themselves, their schools, colleges, their families and friends, and even their country.

We don't share this view at all. We don't believe that all or even most drop-outs are really failures. True, they may for the moment seem to have failed in what they set out to achieve. But our experience over the years tells us that a high percentage will ultimately succeed in school and in life. Some will be even more successful than their friends who finished college on time. We have seen many students dropped from college and have urged others to drop out. We have found that often the act of dropping out of college has forced them to re-examine themselves, their motives, and their values, and has ultimately led them to take the next step with renewed energy and resolution.

You have had your talk with the dean. You are out—temporarily at least. What are you going to do now? That depends very much on whether you are a willing drop-out (WDO) or an unwilling drop-out (UDO).

THE WILLING DROP-OUT

The WDO leaves college of his own free will and with the approval of his dean. Though the WDO may be on mild scholastic probation, his total scholastic standing is usually satisfactory. He is frequently granted a leave of absence and may return in good standing any time he wishes. The WDO leaves for some of the following reasons:

► His academic work is below his expectations.

► He has lost his incentive to study.

► He sees little relation between his studies and the needs of the world around him.

► The Galahad in him makes him want to contribute now to his nation's need through service with the Peace Corps, civil rights groups, etc.

► He wants to get his military obligations behind him.

► He wants to devote a year to intensive study in some area not adequately covered by his college courses, such as music, art, drama.

► His health is poor, or there is serious illness at home.

► His financial problems or those of his parents require a temporary leave.

► He wants to transfer, for good reasons (see page 143).

► He (or she) has married. Girls drop out for this reason more often than boys, though more and more boys and girls are continuing with college after marriage.

If you are a WDO, we assume you have discussed your plans with your parents and your college advisers and instructors. You should also talk with some upperclassmen who have dropped out and returned. You can get the names of such students from your dean. Their experiences can be very useful and revealing.

It is not important that everyone you consult should agree with your decision to drop out. It is important, however, that you confer with older, experienced, balanced, interested people who care about you. After you have listened to everyone, if you still feel that your future growth and development demand that you leave, then leave without feeling proud or guilty or self-righteous. When you resume your studies, they will have more meaning and importance than ever before.

THE UNWILLING DROP-OUT

The UDO has a different problem. He has no choice. He has been asked to leave for one or more of the following reasons:

Academic failure
Misbehavior—cheating, drunkenness, vandalism, etc.
Emotional illness.

If you are a UDO, you may be tempted to blame someone else—your teachers, advisers, fellow students, parents. Don't. Accept your misfortune without bitterness, recrimination, or self-pity. Forget about the past. You can't change it. Hopefully, you won't repeat it. Turn your attention now to some very urgent problems that face you:

How will you break the news to your family? What will you tell them? Don't run away and try to get a job somewhere. This won't solve any of your problems. It won't make you or your parents feel any better. Don't write or wire your parents. Go home and tell them. We know it's hard to confront your parents. But it's the honest and courageous thing to do. In the long run, you'll find it infinitely less painful, too. Of course your parents will be hurt and disappointed. They wouldn't be human if they weren't. But they will understand, as they always have. And they will give you the help, encouragement, and support to work out your plans for the future.

What will you tell your friends, your parents' friends, and your relatives? This is something you and your parents will have to discuss very carefully. Nothing makes a family look more foolish, however, than to have two different stories circulating about why you left college.

Those of your neighbors who are insecure and immature may get some sort of perverse pleasure out of your unhappiness. But the mature and responsible members of your community will understand, knowing that something similar might easily have happened to one of their own.

ACADEMIC FAILURE

If you flunked out of college and you don't know why, now is the time for you to find out. Did you fail because:

You were in the wrong college?

The college expected you to do the kind of work you weren't capable of?

You couldn't keep up with your assignments?

You couldn't understand your professors?

You didn't know how to study?

You spent too much time on social activities, not enough on your studies?

You couldn't get along with the kind of students you found at the college?

You came to college looking for and expecting something the college didn't have?

To get the answers to these and other similar questions, you'll have to do some soul-searching. You may, too, have to call upon deans, teachers, advisers, parents to help you get at the causes of your failure. Without a clear notion of why you failed, you won't be able to make an intelligent come-back.

At this point, a transfer to another college may not necessarily be the best thing for you—particularly if you are planning to take the same kind of program you just failed. This is a very risky move, unless you are sure you know why you failed in your first college and are equally sure that all or most of the elements that led to your failure will not be present in you or in the college you transfer to.

If you failed because you were taking the wrong program, a transfer to another program in another college may make sense. But if your failure lies in your own inadequacies and weaknesses, we suggest you take a year off for a cool, realistic look at yourself. We have found that a year spent working and thinking benefits most students. It gives them what they need at the moment—a change of scene, new insights into themselves, a different outlook on their studies, and a renewed, more meaningful interest in learning.

Frequently the college which dropped you will take you back after a semester or a year, provided you can show that you spent your time away from college constructively, and provided the college is convinced that you have "learned your lesson" and are now ready to meet your obligations as a student and as a citizen.

Before you leave college, confer with your dean about your plans for study and work. At this time, you can make arrangements about when and under what conditions you may be allowed to return. Whatever agreement you reach, ask the dean to confirm it in writing so that there can be no possible misunderstanding in the future. College policies change. Deans move on to other colleges. A written confirmation of your understanding with the dean at the time you leave will be respected and accepted by any college officer when you are ready to return.

DROPPED FOR MISBEHAVIOR

If this is what has happened to you, you will have some difficulty getting into another college. Why? Because you look like a poor risk. Your dismissal may very well have shaken you up and matured you practically overnight, but you are going to have a hard time proving to the colleges that you are really a changed person, worth taking a chance on. Be prepared for a cool and negative reaction from most colleges. But keep on looking and writing and trying. You will, in time, come upon a college that is willing to gamble on you because it feels that you have been punished enough and that you are now really determined to succeed.

EMOTIONAL ILLNESS

Every year a considerable number of students have to drop out of college because they are emotionally disturbed. Their difficulties generally go back some years before they entered college, but in spite of them they managed to hold up remarkably well through high school. Then something in the new demands, new pressures, new environment of college suddenly seems too much, and these students find themselves unable to cope with themselves or their studies.

If emotional problems have forced you to leave college, the first thing you must do is to get the best professional help available as soon as possible. The college medical staff will confer with your parents and your doctor to determine what kind of treatment will be best for you.

Your chances of getting well and back to college again are better than they have ever been. During the past twenty-five years doctors have learned much about the causes of emotional illnesses and have developed great skill in treating them successfully.

So don't get discouraged. We have seen many students

leave college for emotional reasons. Today most of them are leading happy and satisfying lives. They are stronger and more mature because they got the help they needed at the time they needed it.

We hope you will complete your college career on time. But if you have to drop out, don't regard yourself as a failure. Learn from this experience something about yourself, your motives, your standards, ideals, limitations, and foibles. Learn, too, about what the world expects of you.

Dropping out of college is not the end for you. In a very real sense, it may be a beginning—of wisdom, hope, and resolve. Out of your present unhappiness, you will find the strength and the resources to fashion a rich, significant, rewarding life for yourself. It won't be easy. But then what is?

CHAPTER 14

AFTER COLLEGE, WHAT?*

VOCATIONAL dreaming begins early in the life of most men and women. When you were about six years old, success probably meant being a cowboy, a nurse, or a Royal Canadian Mounted Policeman. At ten or eleven you may have thought that the peak of achievement came in directing a jet plane across the ocean, designing a dress, or guiding a submarine under the icy wastelands of the North Pole. Then in early adolescence you imagined yourself a great surgeon, actor, actress, or engineer. Occasionally you permitted yourself to be elected President of the United States. Like Walter Mitty, James Thurber's famous dreamer, all things seemed possible to you. Couldn't any one by hard work and a few breaks be and do anything?

Now that you are in college you see people and jobs more clearly than ever before. Some occupations have become less romantic and less attractive as you learn more about yourself and other people. Perhaps you have discovered that some kinds of thinking and acting come easily to you. Other kinds are difficult or impossible. You realize you cannot be all things to all men. This realization is one sign of maturity.

As you go through four years of college, your vocational

* This chapter is written primarily for students in general education or liberal arts programs, but students in vocationally oriented programs will find it helpful, too.

thinking will be a mixture of dream and reality. In all probability, you will change your vocational goal several times. This change is normal and natural for students with varied aptitudes and interests who are seriously searching for a suitable occupation.

You really have two questions to answer as you face the future. "What am I going to do?" and "Why am I going to do it?" Your college education may suggest that a study of jobs and your interests and aptitudes is not enough. In college, you will be studying ideas as well as techniques, reasons for doing things as well as how to do them. You may find that the question of *why* you want a certain career is even more fundamental than the question of *what* career.

Are you considering a given career because it seems to offer a certain type of social prestige or a certain standard of living? Are you considering it because a parent, relative, or friend wants you to, or because someone you admire has succeeded in it? In this career will you be primarily benefiting yourself, your fellow men, or both—or neither? Does this make a difference to you? Is the purpose served by this career one that can justify it? Will this purpose sustain you through forty years of work? Unless you have faced and answered some of these questions, you aren't ready to choose your lifework intelligently. Your chances for personal satisfaction and therefore for maximum achievement in a given career depend at least as much on the *intent* which lies behind your choice as on the *skills* you master in order to carry it out.

A PLAN FOR ACTION

Somewhere out in the world of work there is the ideal job or career for you. In it you will find all your talents fully employed. You will enjoy every moment. Your fellow workers and employers will recognize your talents. You will be advanced in title and salary a little faster than you deserve. This is the kind of job you dream about and this is the kind of job you hope you will get or be helped into.

There are, however, over 17,000 jobs, careers, professions you could enter. What are your chances of coming upon your dream job? Very slight, indeed. But you can get closer to your heart's desire if you start, as early in college as possible, thinking about what you want to do, why, and how you can best prepare yourself.

The work, time, and thought required for careful career planning should be spread over the four-year college period. Procrastination comes easily to freshmen and sophomores, and especially to those who expect a term of service in the Armed Forces before starting a career. Don't let this anticipated military service stay you from action.

KNOW YOURSELF

Before making a study of occupations, spend some time on a careful analysis of your assets and liabilities. This is not the simple task it seems to be because:

Your vision will probably be blurred when you appraise yourself

Your friends, in a desire to please you, will tend to report only the good.

Make your first observations by yourself and write them down in a notebook. List your observations under three headings: (1) Your physical self, (2) Your intelligence, (3) Your interests.

(1) *Your physical self.* What is your height, weight, endurance? How are your eyes, ears, legs, arms, etc.? Are you clumsy or do you have good physical coordination? Do you like hard physical work?

Some jobs require certain physical qualities. You should consider this when comparing occupations. Make a list of your physical assets and liabilities and don't start on a career in which your advancement may be hampered by some physical limitations.

(2) *Your intelligence.* It is easy to test the strength of your eyes, ears, arms, legs, heart, etc. It is more difficult to estimate your intelligence. We have intelligence tests which reveal your mental age or I.Q., and other tests which indicate your mental abilities in such different areas as space perception, reasoning, mathematics, verbal meanings, word fluency, memory, etc. But many areas remain untested. Such important characteristics as industry, imagination, motivation, and personality cannot yet be measured completely.

I.Q. tests reveal only one thing: how you compare with a cross section of the population in the things tested. A high I.Q. is no guarantee of success, for there are other important qualities which contribute to a man's advancement in his career. Likewise, a low I.Q. does not in itself indicate certain failure.

In most people, areas of intelligence are not evenly distributed. Some have a full measure of verbal intelligence and lack of mathematical intelligence, or vice versa. Some have excellent space perception while others have little or none.

In addition to general intelligence, which is revealed by marks and test scores in school and college, there are two other kinds of intelligence which should be considered. One is social intelligence or the ability to get along with people. Though marks are not given in college for this kind of intelligence, business rates it highly. We all know students who can get high marks but fail completely in activities involving people. The third kind of intelligence might be called "practical intelligence," or the ability to solve certain limited problems of daily living.

Those who are strong in one kind are not superior or inferior to those who possess the others. They are merely different.

It is important to appraise yourself in all three areas because some jobs demand more of one kind of intelligence than another.

(3) *Your interests.* These are many and varied. List all of them, even those which seem to have no bearing on your career. You may have an interest in stamp collecting, birds, jazz records, cooking, or archery. Though these interests are often only hobbies, they can sometimes lead to or suggest the career you should follow.

To uncover your job-related interests, you should answer questions like these: Do you enjoy working with your hands— with motors, wood, metal, television, etc.? Do you like to read and write? Would you rather work inside or outdoors? Do you enjoy working with people—all kinds of people? Do you prefer working alone or in a group? Do you work best under your own planning or under the direction of others?

Tests can be helpful in revealing undiscovered interests and in confirming existing interests. Vocational interest tests will help you compare your interests with those of successful men and women in many occupations. See your counseling staff about such tests.

When you have listed your interests, you must try to determine your aptitude for work in each field. Here your teachers and counselors can be of assistance to you.

Many students have dreamed of being great writers, only to find their abilities unequal to their dreams. Many would-be doctors have foundered on courses in chemistry, would-be engineers on calculus, and would-be personnel managers on human relations.

Finding what you are most interested in is only part of your search for a satisfying career. You must also be reasonably sure that you can do well in what you have chosen.

KNOW ABOUT JOBS

Most people are uncertain about what career they want to pursue because they know very little about the variety and nature of jobs that they are fitted for and would find worth doing.

For instance, if you enjoy group activity, if you are usually successful in your relations with people, you probably think first of careers in selling or personnel. But there are many other jobs that call for an ability to work with people. To mention a few: politics; school and hotel administration; freight and passenger traffic work for bus companies, trucking concerns, railroads, steamships, and airlines; secretarial work; city management; trade associations; merchandising; etc.

If you are good in mathematics, if you enjoy work involving numbers, you may have thought of a teaching career or accounting. But have you investigated such occupations as statistics, actuarial work, computer programming, corporation finance, and investment research?

It is easy to fall into another common error in considering your career. You may think in terms of broad labels rather than specific work. How often have you heard a fellow student say, "I am going into business"? That's as definite as saying, "I'm going to be in Canada," to a friend who wants to know how to reach you during the summer.

More specifically, you might say, "I'm going into advertising." But even here there are subdivisions. Which of the following departments in advertising are you going to enter: art, copy production, marketing, consumer research, radio, television?

Some students profess an interest in sales, but there are sales to consumers, to retailers, wholesalers; sales of tangibles, such as steel, cars, clothing, lumber, etc.; and sales of intangibles, such as insurance, advertising, services, etc.

Teaching is an interesting career to many, but on what

level—kindergarten, elementary, secondary, college, graduate, adult? And in what subject or subjects?

So beware of broad occupational labels. Look behind each to see what its subdivisions are. And try to explore definite jobs, not classifications.

The ideal way to investigate any job is by working in it for a period. But vacations are too few and choices too numerous to permit more than two or three such experiments. This leaves only two avenues of investigation open: reading and talks with jobholders.

Your college library and the placement office have many books that deal with various occupations. Biographies of the successful make interesting and informative reading. Of special interest to you are *Fortune Vocational Index* and *Occupational Outlook Handbook*.

As you appraise different occupations, list in a notebook those which interest you. Then talk to people who are in these occupations about qualifications, educational requirements, salary, opportunities for advancement, etc. You can get introductions through your teachers, the college director of guidance and placement, friends of your father, or fathers of your friends.

Once you have read all you can about a job and talked to people in the job, you should have some idea about your qualifications for and interest in such work, and the employment opportunities. When you begin your investigation of career possibilities, you will find the search interesting and rewarding.

Apply to your career reading and study the same initiative, imagination, and industry you expect to give to your first post-college job. Begin in your freshman year. And follow some systematic timetable, such as the one which follows.

CAREER PLANNING TIMETABLE

FRESHMAN YEAR

1. Begin to study your assets and liabilities, your aptitudes and interests, and write your findings in a notebook.
2. Begin to read about occupations. List those which interest you most.
3. During vacations interview at least one person in each occupation which interests you. (Before discussing an occupation read all you can about it so your interview will be intelligent.)
4. In April or May check your progress with your college's occupational advisers.
5. Try to get a summer job in an occupation which interests you.

SOPHOMORE YEAR AND JUNIOR YEAR

1. Review and revise your appraisal of your assets and liabilities.
2. Continue your exploration of occupations through books, monographs, and articles. Consult the director of guidance and placement, and also faculty specialists about careers in their separate areas.
3. Discuss aptitude and interest tests with occupational advisers or members of the Psychology Department.
4. Discuss your occupational plans with the teacher who has seemed to you to be the best judge of your college work.
5. Use vacations for further interviews with those employed in occupations which interest you.
6. During summer vacation try to get a job in an occupation which interests you. Try to get a different vocational experience each summer. The placement office has files of such opportunities.
7. Watch your college paper for notices of discussions on

careers and of campus visits from representatives of graduate schools and industry. These meetings are open to all students.

8. Attend all career conferences held at your college.

SENIOR YEAR

By the start of senior year you should have a good understanding of your strengths and weaknesses, your aptitudes and interests. You should also know the kind of work you want and for which you are qualified. If you are going to graduate school, you should know how and when to apply to the school of your choice. Get information and advice from appropriate members of the faculty.

If you are going into business, read materials on the techniques of job getting. Discuss your vocational decisions with the director of guidance and placement. Have interviews with company personnel officers and deans of graduate schools who come to the campus during the winter and spring for recruiting purposes. Use vacation time for job-seeking interviews.

WHERE TO GET CAREER INFORMATION

Write to the organizations listed here if you are interested in any of the following careers. They will send you materials describing the nature of the work, the kind of preparation needed, where to get the necessary training, where jobs can be found, employment prospects, starting salaries, opportunities for advancement, etc.

ACCOUNTANT

American Institute of Certified Public Accountants
270 Madison Avenue, New York, N.Y.

National Association of Accountants
505 Park Avenue, New York, N.Y.

Controllers Institute of America
2 Park Avenue, New York, N.Y.

The Institute of Internal Auditors
120 Wall Street, New York, N.Y.

ACTUARY

Society of Actuaries
208 South LaSalle Street, Chicago, Ill.

Casualty Actuarial Society
200 East 42 Street, New York, N.Y.

ADVERTISING

Advertising Federation of America
655 Madison Avenue, New York, N.Y.

American Association of Advertising Agencies
420 Lexington Avenue, New York, N.Y.

Association of National Advertisers
155 East 44 Street, New York, N.Y.

AGRICULTURE

U.S. Department of Agriculture
Washington, D.C.

ANTHROPOLOGIST

American Anthropological Association
1530 P Street NW, Washington, D.C.

American Sociological Association
New York University,
Washington Square, New York, N.Y.

ARCHAEOLOGIST

American Anthropological Association
1530 P Street NW, Washington, D.C.

American Historical Association
400 A Street SE, Washington, D.C.

ARCHITECT

American Institute of Architects
1735 New York Avenue NW, Washington, D.C.

ASTRONOMER

American Astronomical Society
Dearborn Observatory,
Northwestern University, Evanston, Ill.

BACTERIOLOGIST

American Institute of Biological Sciences
2000 P Street NW, Washington, D.C.

Federation of American Societies for Experimental Biology
9650 Wisconsin Avenue NW, Washington, D.C.

BANKING

American Bankers Association
12 East 36 Street, New York, N.Y.

BIOLOGIST

American Institute of Biological Sciences
2000 P Street NW, Washington, D.C.

Federation of American Societies for Experimental Biology
9650 Wisconsin Avenue NW, Washington, D.C.

Office of Personnel, U.S. Department of Agriculture
Washington, D.C.

Employment Officer, U.S. Department of Health, Education and Welfare
National Institute of Health, Bethesda, Md.

BIOPHYSICIST

American Institute of Biological Sciences
2000 P Street NW, Washington, D.C.

Federation of American Societies for Experimental Biology
9650 Wisconsin Avenue NW, Washington, D.C.

BOTANIST

American Institute of Biological Sciences
2000 P Street NW, Washington, D.C.

CHEMIST

American Chemical Society
1155 16 Street NW, Washington, D.C.

Manufacturing Chemists Association, Inc.
1825 Connecticut Avenue NW, Washington, D.C.

CHIROPODIST

American Podiatry Association
3301 16 Street NW, Washington, D.C.

CHIROPRACTOR

International Chiropractors Association
741 Brady Street, Davenport, Iowa

National Chiropractic Association
National Building, Webster City, Iowa

COMMERCIAL ARTIST

National Society of Art Directors
115 East 40 Street, New York, N.Y.

National Association of Schools of Art
50 Astor Place, New York, N.Y.

DENTAL HYGIENIST

American Dental Hygienists' Association
100 East Ohio Street, Chicago, Ill.

DENTAL LABORATORY TECHNICIAN

American Dental Association, Council on Dental Education
222 East Superior Street, Chicago, Ill.

National Association of Dental Laboratories
201 Mills Building, Washington, D.C.

DENTIST

American Dental Association, Council on Dental Education
222 East Superior Street, Chicago, Ill.

DESIGNER

Apparel

Amalgamated Clothing Workers of America
15 Union Square, New York, N.Y.

Clothing Manufacturers Association of U.S.A.
230 Fifth Avenue, New York, N.Y.

International Ladies' Garment Workers' Union
1710 Broadway, New York, N.Y.

United Garment Workers of America
31 Union Square, New York, N.Y.

Industrial

American Society of Industrial Designers
15 East 48 Street, New York, N.Y.

Industrial Designers' Institute
441 Madison Avenue, New York, N.Y.

Interior

American Institute of Interior Designers
673 Fifth Avenue, New York, N.Y.

National Society of Interior Designers, Inc.
Suite 700, 157 West 57 Street, New York, N.Y.

DRAFTSMAN

American Federation of Technical Engineers
900 F Street NW, Washington, D.C.

DIETITIAN

American Dietetic Association
620 North Michigan Avenue, Chicago, Ill.

DOCTOR

Council on Medical Education and Hospitals
American Medical Association
535 Dearborn Street, Chicago, Ill.

Association of American Medical Colleges
2530 Ridge Avenue, Evanston, Ill.

ECONOMIST

American Economic Association
Northwestern University, Evanston, Ill.

National Council of Technical Schools
1507 M Street NW, Washington, D.C.

ENGINEER

Technical Institute Division
American Society for Engineering Education
University of Illinois, Urbana, Ill.

Engineers Council for Professional Development
345 East 47 Street, New York, N.Y.

Engineers Joint Council
345 East 47 Street, New York, N.Y.

National Society of Professional Engineers
2029 K Street NW, Washington, D.C.

American Ceramic Society
4055 North High Street, Columbus, Ohio

American Institute of Chemical Engineers
345 East 47 Street, New York, N.Y.

American Institute of Electrical Engineers
345 East 47 Street, New York, N.Y.

American Institute of Industrial Engineers
145 North High Street, Columbus, Ohio

American Institute of Mining, Metallurgical and Petroleum Engineers
345 East 47 Street, New York, N.Y.

American Society of Civil Engineers
345 East 47 Street, New York, N.Y.

American Society of Mechanical Engineers
345 East 47 Street, New York, N.Y.

Institute of the Aerospace Sciences, Inc.
2 East 64 Street, New York, N.Y.

ENGINEERING TECHNICIAN

Engineers Council for Professional Development
345 East 47 Street, New York, N.Y.

Technical Institute Division
American Society for Engineering Education
University of Illinois, Urbana, Ill.

National Council of Technical Schools
1507 M Street NW, Washington, D.C.

American Association of Junior Colleges
1785 Massachusetts Avenue NW, Washington, D.C.

F.B.I. AGENT

Federal Bureau of Investigation, U.S. Department of Justice
Washington, D.C.

FEDERAL GOVERNMENT SERVICE
U.S. Civil Service Commission
Washington, D.C.

FOOD MANAGER

Hotel

American Hotel and Motel Association
221 West 57 Street, New York, N.Y.

Council on Hotel, Restaurant, and Institutional Education
Statler Hall, Cornell University, Ithaca, N.Y.

Restaurant

Educational Director, National Restaurant Association
1530 North Lake Shore Drive, Chicago, Ill.

Council on Hotel, Restaurant, and Institutional Education
Statler Hall, Cornell University, Ithaca, N.Y.

FORESTER
Society of American Foresters
425 Mills Building
17 Street and Pennsylvania Avenue NW, Washington, D.C.

Forest Service, U.S. Department of Agriculture
Washington, D.C.

American Forest Products Industries, Inc.
1816 N Street NW, Washington, D.C.

National Lumber Manufacturers Association
1319 18 Street NW, Washington, D.C.

GEOLOGIST
American Geological Institute
2101 Constitution Avenue NW, Washington, D.C.

GEOPHYSICIST
American Geophysical Union
1515 Massachusetts Avenue NW, Washington, D.C.

Society of Exploration Geophysicists
Box 1536, Tulsa, Okla.

HISTORIAN

American Historical Association
400 A Street SE, Washington, D.C.

HOME ECONOMIST

American Home Economics Association
1600 20 Street NW, Washington, D.C.

HOSPITAL ADMINISTRATION

American College of Hospital Administrators
840 North Lake Shore Drive, Chicago, Ill.

HOTEL MANAGER

Council on Hotel, Restaurant, and Institutional Education
Statler Hall, Cornell University, Ithaca, N.Y.

INSURANCE

Institute of Life Insurance
488 Madison Avenue, New York, N.Y.

Insurance Information Institute
110 William Street, New York, N.Y.

LAWYER

American Bar Association
1155 East 60 Street, Chicago, Ill.

LEGAL SECRETARY

United Business Schools Association
1518 K Street NW, Washington, D.C.

LIBRARIAN

American Library Association
50 East Huron Street, Chicago, Ill.

MATHEMATICIAN

American Mathematical Society
190 Hope Street, Providence, R.I.

Mathematical Association of America
University of Buffalo, Buffalo, N.Y.

MEDICAL RECORD LIBRARIAN

American Association of Medical Record Librarians
840 North Shore Drive, Chicago, Ill.

MEDICAL X-RAY TECHNICIAN

American Registry of X-Ray Technicians
2600 Wayzata Boulevard, Minneapolis, Minn.

American Society of X-Ray Technicians
16 14 Street, Fond du Lac, Wis.

MEDICAL TECHNOLOGIST

Registry of Medical Technologists
American Society of Clinical Pathologists
P.O. Box 44, Muncie, Ind.

American Society of Medical Technologists
Suite 25, Hermann Professional Building, Houston, Tex.

METEOROLOGIST

American Meteorological Society
45 Beacon Street, Boston, Mass.

NEWSPAPER REPORTER

American Newspaper Publishers Association
750 Third Avenue, New York, N.Y.

The Newspaper Fund, Inc.
44 Broad Street, New York, N.Y.

NURSE

National League for Nursing
10 Columbus Circle, New York, N.Y.

OCCUPATIONAL THERAPIST

American Occupational Therapy Association
250 West 57 Street, New York, N.Y.

OCEANOGRAPHER

American Society of Limnology and Oceanography
Sapelo Island Research Foundation
Sapelo Island, Ga.

Interagency Committee on Oceanography
Room 1714, Building T-3, 17 Street and Constitution Avenue NW,
Washington, D.C.

OPTOMETRIST

American Optometric Association, Inc.
4030 Chouteau Avenue, St. Louis, Mo.

PHARMACIST

American Pharmaceutical Association
2215 Constitution Avenue NW, Washington, D.C.

PHOTOGRAPHER

Professional Photographers of America, Inc.
152 West Wisconsin Avenue, Milwaukee, Wis.

PHYSICAL THERAPIST

American Physical Therapy Association
1790 Broadway, New York, N.Y.

PHYSICIST

American Institute of Physics
335 East 45 Street, New York, N.Y.

PILOT, FLIGHT ENGINEER

Correspondence Inquiry Branch, MS-126, Federal Aviation Agency
Washington, D.C.

POLITICAL SCIENTIST

American Political Science Association
1726 Massachusetts Avenue NW, Washington, D.C.

PSYCHOLOGIST

American Psychological Association
1333 16 Street NW, Washington, D.C.

PUBLIC RELATIONS

Public Relations Society of America, Inc.
375 Park Avenue, New York, N.Y.

SOCIAL WORKER

Council on Social Work Education
345 East 46 Street, New York, N.Y.

National Association of Social Workers
95 Madison Avenue, New York, N.Y.

SOCIOLOGIST

American Sociological Association
New York University,
Washington Square, New York, N.Y.

STATISTICIAN

American Statistical Association
1757 K Street NW, Washington, D.C.

SURVEYOR

American Congress on Surveying and Mapping
Woodward Building, Washington, D.C.

American Society of Photogrammetry
44 Leesburg Pike, Falls Church, Va.

TEACHER

U.S. Department of Health, Education and Welfare
Washington, D.C.

National Education Association
1201 16 Street NW, Washington, D.C.

American Association of University Professors
1785 Massachusetts Avenue NW, Washington, D.C.

American Council on Education
1785 Massachusetts Avenue NW, Washington, D.C.

Board of Education of your town or city.

State Education Department in the capital of your state.

VETERINARIAN

American Veterinary Medical Association
600 South Michigan Avenue, Chicago, Ill.